"*It would take a trainer like yourself to put something together that really makes sense to the general public. I like it alot.*" - Lee Sollenberger (Grizzly Adams, Animal trainer)

THE DOG'S HONEST TRUTH

The Dog's Honest Truth
Copyright © Gary Jackson, 2013

First published 2013

Published by Cobble Hill Publishing
4445 Trans Canada Highway,
Cobble Hill, Canada, V0R1L0
Email: garyrjackson@gmail.com
Phone: 1.250.709.3757
URL: http://www.jacksontraining.ca

Original photographs by: Sondercroft

Printed by Cobble Hill Publishing
The Dog's Honest Truth
Jackson, Gary

ISBN: 978-0-9921450-0-2
                    Electronic format
                    E-ISBN: 978-0-9921450-1-9

This book is dedicated with love to:

Allie, Sydni, Emma and Connor, the most incredible children ever.

Special thanks to Judy Pigott for her fine job of editting, any errors or grammatical transgressions that remain are solely my doing. My gratitude to Gerry for all your one-liners and challenges.

Most of all, to Grandpa. You were right.

CONTENTS

INTRODUCTION

The Dog's Honest Truth is a collection of animal stories linked together with bits of grassroots training philosophy and how-to instruction. It debunks the myth of "alpha" based approaches in dog training and points to a way of training that is nurturing and natural - for dogs and ourselves.

The Author ,Gary Jackson, has spent a lifetime training horses and dogs in the private sector. In 1988 his animal training talents were recruited and put to the test on movies like: Grey Owl, The Bone Collector and The Grey. The insights he gained from working hands-on with wolves and other wild and domestic species helped create his unique philosophy that has empowered pet owners for over twenty-five years.

Dedicated to humane animal treatment, Gary spent almost ten years as a Special Provincial Constable for the BCSPCA, investigating animal cruelty and enforcing provincial and federal animal protection laws. During this time he became aware of the plight of homeless animals. Resources to address these animal's behavioural problems were few and far between which motivated his development of a behavioural rehabilitation facility that deals with last-chance dogs and hopeless owners.

The Dog's Honest Truth offers simple solutions and gives pet owners ways in which to embody their animal's point of view so they might better empathize and humanely provide for their dog's physical and emotional needs.The Dog's Honest Truth asks that we learn nothing new, but simply acknowledge and relate to other species through the *animal* in us all. Common challenges including: leash pulling, possessiveness, anxiety or aggression are dissected. By understanding the origin of each *problem* behaviour the solutions become clear.

Perspective, gives us an understanding of an other's physical needs and more importantly, it allows us to empathize with their emotional needs. Communication skills, help forge the bond that blooms into trust, rapport and self-motivated '*obedience*.' The Dog's Honest Truth gives new and experienced dog owners the opportunity to take a walk on the (almost) wild side.

CHAPTER ONE

The Truth About Dogs

Perspective

Porter

The woman, in her early 30's, gripped her dog's leash with white knuckles. Her eyes sought reassurance from me, as I walked toward where they stood waiting. A big, 3 year old American Bulldog strained on the rope and dared me to come closer. He snarled, barked, and grumbled low growls. He held his head low and stared up at me with a cool rage. I had a pretty good feeling that he wasn't joking.

When I brought out my four hundred pound bodyguard, named Hawg, the bulldog couldn't have cared less. Hawg is a pig I've raised from a baby to work as my helper. The dog didn't mind when Hawg bumped him out of the way to get a piece of bread. He just wanted me close enough so he could get a good hold!

* * *

His name was Porter and he'd run the gauntlet of Victoria, BC's trainers and behaviour specialists. His owners had sent video, letters, and telephone pleas to all the top dog experts on TV. First, asking for help, and then begging. It seemed no one could touch him let alone fix him.

Porter hadn't always been a 'man-eater'. Footage they had from when he was younger showed a well-balanced, socially appropriate and intelligent dog. They'd taught him a whack of parlour tricks and all his obedience commands. Still, something had gone wrong and Porter was one of the most dangerous dogs I'd seen. I was reluctant, but admitted him for rehabilitation with a guarded prognosis.

After two months, and different reasons, his people were forced to give up on him. Rather than quit along with them, I let him stay. He was still aggressive beyond reason, triggered with the slightest look or posture. Porter was dangerous, but fascinating. In two months he hadn't softened in the least: not for food, nor company. He was determined to hate my guts.

Porter was housed in a kennel at night, and spent his days in a fenced swimming pool area next to the house. When he was dropped off he had been fitted with an appropriate collar with a six foot, coated cable attached. Every day I'd crack his kennel door, hook the cable attached to his collar with a cane, and then clip it to a cotton long line. This allowed him to 'run away' when I turned him out of the kennel. Cane in hand, we'd make our way through the yard to the pool. The walk always felt - touch and go. Porter was barely able to stand my presence.

Two months turned into three and then four. Nothing changed. He never 'attacked' and I never had to use the cane for anything, other than hooking the cable to bring him out of his kennel. We'd reached an uneasy truce, a stalemate.

By the fifth month of this back and forth, going nowhere, I was questioning myself. My friends and acquaintances were beginning to shake their heads. Yet, for no other reason than a "little voice" in my head, I stuck with Porter. The little voice's message was consistent, yet vague. "Something will happen!"

By month six of our daily walks to nowhere, I began wondering who was more messed up - the dog or me! Common sense and logic would dictate that if, 'something-will-happen' were going to happen, it would have happened a long time ago.

Then the morning came when I turned him into the pool area and went into the house for a coffee. I'd made it into the kitchen when I heard Porter erupt into panicked barks. "Woo-woo, woo-woo-woo, woo-wooo-ooo-ooo!"

"*Something* is happening!" that little inside-voice said.

I was through the gate, running around behind Porter,

before I realized "Oops! No Cane!"

It was too late to retreat, though I hadn't been sure what it was that I was going to do once I was in there! Then I saw what was scaring the bejeezus out of him. It was all I could do not to howl with laughter.

We'd had a deluge of summer-company that year, and the pool had been well used. The kids had had an assortment of water toys in the pool. One of the toys was a little cartoon dinosaur looking thing, that a small child might float on.

For whatever reason, after months of sharing the same space, Porter had looked into the pool at just the right time to see the wind pushing this nasty looking 'monster' toward him in the water. Big round eyes stared at him, sharp white teeth pointed in his direction, and the monster floated closer and closer.

Porter was terrified!

As the dinosaur bore down on Porter, I stood in front of him, and to his right. The lobe of the kidney shaped pool circled between us. The water was well below the pavement level, so when the toy floated up against the side of the pool, it disappeared from Porter's line of sight. I'd stopped right where the toy made land fall. A total fluke!

Porter was still in panic mode, barking, hackles raised, his eyes dilated to black. Poor bugger really thought his time had come. He couldn't see the monster anymore, but he knew it was there, just out of his sight.

I knelt down, reached for the toy, and grasped its tail.

"*Something is Happening*" chuckled my little inside-voice.

I did what any primate would do when confronted with a terrified animal. I scared him some more!

I flipped the dinosaur up out of the water. It landed right at Porter's feet. Luck was with us that morning. It came to rest right-side-up, facing Porter with those big eyes and teeth. Ready to eat him up!

I didn't know a dog could back up that fast. He skittered backwards and came to a stop only when his arse hit the fence.

Then he froze, not knowing what to do. This dog, that had nerves of steel when challenging a human, had been stopped cold by a blow-up toy!

I now got an idea of what that "something" might be that my little inside-voice had been talking about. I stood up and walked to where the attack dinosaur threatened the big bulldog.

I pounced on it, ripped it from the ground, and did a very convincing job of beating the crap out of the monster. I ended with pretending to bite its face, and then threw it back in the water. Luck still with us, it landed belly up! I turned my puffed up, dinosaur killing posture to Porter, who'd watched it all in silence. His front legs still splayed, his eyes round, Porter was a hopeless, cornered animal full of disbelief and fear.

When we made eye contact, he said his first 'nice' words to me in six months.

Porter dropped into a play-bow, curled his butt around to show me how low his tail was, and in as many ways as a dog can without words said "Wow man! That was great! How'd you do that! Can I be your pal?"

After six months of no forced physical contact, training, or corrections, the dog no one could touch had his breakthrough.

He'd witnessed someone be more 'powerful' in a situation where he had found himself overwhelmed with fear and doubt. He had seen someone be 'bigger' than he thought himself ever capable of being, and cast his lot and allegiance to that person. He made the decision himself. His perspective was changed by watching, not by being forced or 'broken'.

Within ten minutes of killing the dinosaur, I sat on the diving board with Porter beside me, leaning his weight, and slobbering his appreciation all over me. The past 6 months had been erased from his mind with the death of a blow-up floaty toy.

The other trainers had tried to change the animal's

actions, when all Porter needed was to have his mind changed first.

We should be grateful that dogs like Porter, are few and far between.

Most clients arrive with dogs that are far less dramatic in their behaviours than Porter. Many have reached the point where they are on their last chance, after repeated bites or maulings. Many believe their dog is a monster for snacking on the neighbour's rabbits, or for catching the slow old hen. Some dogs are not aggressive, but stress ridden and twitchy as a meth-head. Like Porter and his people, they all share a common plight – cataracts. Not the white cloudy eye disease, but cataracts that cloud, both the human's, and animal's vision surrounding their relation with one another and the outside world.

At an industrial level, there are so few dogs that could be labelled "Unpredictable" or "Beyond Redemption," that I wonder at their real existence in the first place. If we compare those rare "mad dogs" to our own society's mental health issues, we'd have to concede that erratic behaviour, unbeatable compulsion, aggression, depression, and phobias, are more the province of our own species than that of our animals'.

For clients that show up here, regardless of their crisis, the resolution is consistently the same. This is where we'll pick up the story and shoot for the human/dog panacea for relationships, that is *clear perspective* - the dog's honest truth.

Bursting Bubbles

The beginning of each session is the same. Most people and their dogs live urban or semi-urban lives. Their worlds revolve around the click and whir of this busy modern society. When they hit the ground, here on the farm, they experience a sensory overload that takes a few minutes for them to adjust to. Their senses take command while they check-out the foreign new environment. During the time they're 'overwhelmed' a clear picture of how the dog and owner get along is painted.

As the dog's mind settles, it's eyes, ears, and nose release control after having high-jacked its motor functions, while they carry out their 'recon' of the new surroundings. We then introduce the dog to more new things. The stimulus might be something small, like a cat or chicken, or something big and intimidating, like a full grown hog or a horse. It all depends on what the dog says with its body language. How it responds to these stressors provides insight into the way it views the world around it, and gives a good indication of how it will react under extreme stress.

At the same time the dog is being assessed, the owners show their own level of confidence or unease, and how they interact with their dog in uncertain times. Most valuable, during this initial greeting, is the depiction of the relationship between human and canine. The whole process only lasts a few minutes. Then the dog is put away. The clients are led into the house and seated at a table with a single piece of paper and a pen.

When it comes to sitting down with the people, no matter what their dog's problem, the single piece of paper and what's drawn on it doesn't change. It's sort of a quick-start owner's manual. All the information is there, it just depends on how well you know the general workings of the machine.

The efficacy of this format is its simplicity. It uses common emotions and behaviours that we can all relate to, dog or human. In essence: emotions or behaviours older than we are as a species - common ground.

The human lesson starts with a question: "What kind of dog do you have to act like, for your dog to listen to you?"

"The Alpha!" they answer.

I only let them be a little right. I'm a tough trainer - but I make damn good coffee, so they take it!

I explain to them that the perspective of "Alpha" is correct, for most canines. I'll draw them a Christmas tree with a few rows of garland, a trunk, and a hole in the ground at the base of the tree. I'm a poor artist, so when I start doodling, their faces sometimes show a little concern, nonverbally expressing their thoughts that say, "What the...!?" Above the tree, before they get up to leave, I write the word ALPHA. I reiterate that yes, alpha is the accepted terminology used to define the upper tier of canine society.

It goes like this:

The closest wild relative to modern dog is the wolf. If we look at the organization of a wolf pack, there are two Alpha animals, the Male and the Female. It's possible that, from this canine analogy, we get some male-based 'hope' for touting our own views of a patriarchal society.

The alpha-male wolf, that big intimidating creature from nursery rhymes and horror movies, has to be the leader.
Right! Right?

Only "Partly" right. The Alpha-male is merely the Big Girl's henchman. Yes, he has the physical ability to overpower her, dominate her, if you will. But for the most part, he doesn't. She has the most important role in the pack. Her reign and dominion include, producing the young, nurturing them, teaching them what they will need to know to be contributing members, supervising their play and exploration, guarding against predation, all the while maintaining peace and equanimity among the other pack members. The only time the big guy steps up to the plate, is if one of the subdominant animals gives her too much 'back-talk'. Otherwise, he's happy lording over his group from a quiet patch of sunshine.

The illustration of the Christmas tree, drawn on the paper, depicts the pyramidal structure of a wild canine pack. There are more animals on the subdominant levels than there are nearer the top of the tree. Individuals behave differently toward members they perceive as equals, compared to those they see as more or less dominant.

The only animals in a wild pack that live outside this societal structure are the pups. From the time they're ready to leave the den, at three and a half weeks of age, they have a clear line through the pack to where their momma is, and that's usually not too far away. If the pups' Aunt Gert happens to be lying in the middle of the clearing, and little Jake starts toddling her way, she'll be up and out of his way before the little tyke has a chance to step on her tail or bite her ear. She doesn't want to be anywhere near the little guy if he starts crying! She knows the Big Girl will "Come down hard" on whoever is closest to her crying pup! This isn't something that Gert learnt through trial and error. Most adult male dogs will react with the same aversion to pups as she does.

If we place a pup beside a sleeping old dog, we can trigger this same instinct. When he notices the wee one, the old guy will retreat from the squirming little infant intruder as if to say, "Aargh! GET AWAY - COOTIES!!"

Ben, a lab/rottie cross, was a stellar work dog, socialized, and rock stable under any imaginable situation. His kryptonite was any unweaned pup. This big old dog would turn himself inside out and jiggle away at the first sight of an infant pup. He'd stop at a distance and turn around, keeping his eye on the pup. He'd bounce on his front legs with his lips pulled tight, ears back, tail low and wagging fast. All his language systems projected the stress he felt being near such a small one. It seems that, regardless of species, every animal knows: Don't Mess With The Momma! If there's smoke there's fire! If there's a pup...!

Once in a while you will find a male that goes against this tendency, but not often.

Luke was a shepherd that broke this rule. If you put anything small and helpless in front of him, he was on duty. He'd fret and group, lick and organize, incessantly. Each squeak treated with a nose-bump or a sniff. He'd get a creased brow and worried look in his eye until he could position his charges between his front legs. All accounted for, he would glow with purpose.

Female animals, Domestic or Wild, are a more complex creature than their male counterparts. Their aversion, or non-aversion to small pups, varies depending on the individual.

Spayed domestic females can be hot or cold with pups. Some are as repulsed by pups as many males are. Others seem to be flooded with maternal hormones at just a glimpse of a pup. It's amazing to see a never-bred female begin sympathetic lactation and perform motherly tasks for surrogate pups.

In wild canines, behaviour surrounding young pups in a pack is straight forward and predictable. From 3 1/2 weeks until the pups are 3 or 4 months of age, nobody will have much to do with them: 'the seas part' - kind of thing.

They have a clear route to mom at all times. As they develop, growing in size and maturity, they begin to explore their expanded 'wolf' society. There comes a day when stepping on Aunt Gert's tail, in the middle of a tussle, gets rambunctious siblings a growl and a snap, as the old wolf moves away from the heathen pair. Big Momma only responds with a cursory glance at the proceedings, and ignores the senior wolf's correction of her pups. It's a slippery slope for the pups from there, and soon the whole 'community' is helping to raise the pups, instilling manners and expectations, and unspoken rules and constraints on acceptable behaviours.

Domestic pups follow a similar developmental curve, for those first few months. The difference between wild and domestic infants becomes stark between 4 - 7 months. At this point domestic dog's mental maturity starts to plateau. The wild ones will continue to mature for a much longer time.

Our domestic pups never attain the 'wisdom' achieved by their wild counterparts. They'll never be able to, confidently or with much degree of certainty, control a group of their peers, let alone orchestrate (in the same efficient way as wolves) a successful hunt involving larger prey. That's not to say dog predation isn't common, and its toll on farmer's stocks are not considerable. It does happen. Single or groups of domestic canines will band together and perform all out assaults: demolishing entire herds of sheep, goats, or fowl, without feeding on any single one: holes torn in necks, severed leg tendons, or dead, without a mark from being chased to death.

By comparison, wolves use almost surgical precision in every aspect of their hunts: search, stalking abilities, selection of prey, and execution of the capture. Their domestic counterparts can only respond to clouded ancient instincts, and 'imagine' how it really works in the world of their wild relatives.

From urbane outlooks, it's easy to overlook the most primal forces driving our canine fellows. In the great span of time, since their domestication, we as a race have changed the face of the planet. But, we're the only species that understands why. Our dogs cannot grasp the realities of their keepers, nor their ancestors. Domestication was the culprit!

Domestication

From: do mes ti cate (d-mst-kt)
tr.v. do mes ti cat ed, do mes ti cat ing, do mes ti cates
1. To cause to feel comfortable at home; make domestic
2. To adopt or make fit for domestic use or life
3. a. To train or adapt (an animal or plant) to live in a human environment and be of use to humans
b. To introduce and accustom (an animal or plant) into another region; naturalize
4. To bring down to the level of the ordinary person.
n. (-kt, -kt)
A plant or animal, that has been adapted to living in a human environment.

* * *

After the picture of the tree is all nicely drawn and decorated, clients are asked to ponder: What do all of man's domestic animals have in common?

The answer: They all originate from wild ancestors with social species backgrounds.

Whether it's a chicken, goat, sheep, or dog: whether it's a prey animal or a predator, their roots in the wild included them spending much of their time looking at others who looked much the same as they did.

The process that turned wolves into dogs is believed to have happened over centuries.

A study performed, with Silver Fox in the 1950s', showed that the process of domestication could have occurred within a relatively short span of time.

Silver fox are born mottle coloured. Over the course of 5 years they grow and mature, with their coats turning silver as they achieve maturity. A fur-bearing mammal, they were highly prized and bred extensively, similar to members of the ermine family in Canada and the United States. These animals required daily cleaning and feeding, while living in cramped quarters. The labour cost of producing one silver fox pelt was staggering and time consuming. A captive breeding program was initiated, with the hopes of domesticating the fox, enabling it to be housed and cared for under less demanding circumstances.

* * *

In ten generations of captive breeding, they attained the behavioural changes that were desired.

A black and white documentary film was released, showing the results. A mottled fox ran around a barnyard full of other domestic animals. The fox was obviously enjoying itself, and used pup-like behaviour as a means of communicating its feelings. It circled a turkey. Bolted behind a sheep, and reappeared beside a donkey. A toddler was standing beside a water trough splashing the surface, the fox ended the scene by grabbing the infant's diaper, instigating a playful game of tug-o-war.

For all intents and purposes, the breeding program appeared to have succeeded in its goals.

There was a drawback. The fox's behaviour was dog-like. In every sense it was as gentle, malleable, and dependant as a domestic dog. With its puppy-like behaviour and mottled colouring, the animal appeared to be a normal immature fox, except well adapted to humans. What was amiss was that the animal in the film was a 6 year old female. She stayed 'nice' throughout her life, but never turned silver in colour. Her immature behaviour into adulthood seemed to affect her coloration. Neither her mind, nor her coat ever matured to normal adult standards.

Those of us, who have had the good fortune to work with social species of both domestic, and wild origin, have an easier time understanding the range of differences between wild and domestic animals. When experienced first-hand, the changes that occur during development within a wild mammal brain compared to their domestic cousins, is stark and undeniable.

Ben

Ben was a good old dog. His repertoire of parlour tricks, directional commands, and trained behaviours was vast. Aside from being a good working dog, he was an exceptional family pet. He lived indoors, among our four children, and was a trusted companion. He knew all the "do's and don'ts" of being a house dog, and was in every way a great mutt.

He lived to be 14 years old. Two weeks prior to his death, he suffered a minor stroke that effected his motor skills and energy levels. He recovered slowly, but he was only comfortable going outside for a few minutes at a time, before wanting back inside to lay by the wood-stove. His last day on earth was a rainy one. I let him out for his morning pee and, after 20 minutes, realized with a feeling of dread, that he should have been back scratching at the door to come in. As I passed the picture window, I saw him in the middle of the lawn.

The old dog had decided to have a final hoorah!

The night before, we'd left a shopping bag on the table beside the barbecue. Inside it were the empty meat wrappers that had carried our steaks. Even though Benny knew, for more than a decade, that garbage wasn't something he should get into, he had taken the bag off the table and carried it out onto the lawn. When I spotted him, he was absorbed in tossing it up in the air, trying to get the contents to fall out. I'm sure he was thinking he'd be okay, as long as he didn't destroy the bag (carrying a shopping bag home from the store had been a favourite job of his, in earlier days).

Seeing the old dog acting like a carefree pup, struck a chord in me. I stayed in the house and let him enjoy his trophy. I'll always be grateful that I did. It wasn't long before he accomplished what he had set out to do, and was scratching at the door, not a bit of guilt or apprehension showing in his countenance. A well-licked pile of butcher's paper waved from the lawn. He was satisfied.

Two hours later, while I wrote at the computer, I heard him give a couple of quick, deep breaths. He had done that kind of thing before, so that time I'd paid no attention. When I got up, a little while later, I discovered that my old friend had died right beside me. His old body had had a good last fling, and then waited till the old guy was sleeping to shut down for good.

Ben's story epitomizes the effects of domestication on our canine breeds. Up until his last day, he performed 'pup-like' behaviours, doing something he knew was taboo, in spite of learned consequences. The youthful joy he procured by tossing the bag in the air, rather than shredding it, can only be compared to an adolescent attempt at subverting parental or societal constraints, even though they are likely to be caught. It seems, programmed within social species animals, that youths must test and re-test authority.

It could be argued that dementia may have been a factor in Ben's immature 'lapse' in judgement, but no mental declines were noticeable. He relished being asked to do a job, like closing the door, or bringing something to me, his behaviour with other dogs remained the same, as was every other part of his personality. His body was the only thing that failed him.

All of our domestic dogs possess their own personalities and sets of talents, that are linked to their wolf-pasts. Each breed of dog was selectively bred to highlight traits or skills that were beneficial to their human keepers. The adage "We can't escape our past" is true for them in this regard. But the most important truth to acknowledge is our own roll in what we've done to create these malleable wolf look-a-likes.

We've literally retarded their ability to mentally mature.

The Muted Wolf

Social species animals, prey or predator, wild or domestic, have more psychological similarities than they have dissimilarities. A short overview would include that they all:
- Thrive within a hierarchy
- Use language within their social groups
- Feel uncomfortable isolated from their peers

21

- Depend on others to provide some of their emotional and physiological needs

If we look through early man's eyes, the reasons for choices they made, selecting species for domestication becomes clearer. They could decipher the animal's language, and predict future behaviour and movements. They could anticipate the animal's needs, and create ways of communicating with them that resulted in reliable responses. They drew these early conclusions, based on their own experiences as a social species animal. They could empathize and anticipate the actions of a different species, because they could effectively "put their feet in another's shoes".

They could identify the meaning behind their behaviours, and the things that motivated them, because they too were a social species animal. We're all drawn to company of our own kind, and find comfort in the presence of those we're close to. We are all motivated through instinctual social needs that, once met, provide us with a sense of wellbeing and emotional fulfillment.

Physically, animal brains are similar to our own, but they lack the huge prefrontal cortex with which our species is endowed. This difference in brain structure separates us from all other species of mammals. It allows us to use language, have the rare ability of self-perception, and abstract thought. We can envision, create ideas, and inhibit our actions and emotions: whereas our domestic animals are said to have less cognition, fore-thought, and creativity. Many people deny the innate cognitive

22

functions of <u>lesser</u> animals. We human beings are a racy lot. We want to be smarter, stronger, and faster. We're the top of the food chain and we want to stay there!

In reality, those 'lesser' animals we lord-over are endowed with 'different' talents that we can only wish for. Current views rate self-perception and spoken language as the benchmark of intelligence, to which we hold up all other species...

That's a pretty safe thing to do, if you want to stay on top. Pick something few of the others can do, and wave it around in front of their noses. If we turned the tables, and put hearing and scenting as the measure for supreme intelligence, wouldn't we be screwed?

Thankfully, it's not a race and we still reign supreme. We can put away our competitive side and appreciate other animals for the whole and perfect adaptations that they are. We can relish other species talents, language, and behaviours and allow them to compliment and enrich our existence. In this way we can enjoy deeper and more natural experiences in our multi-species relationships.

To make this shift in perspective we have to wade through the quagmire of our current social views on animals. The demographics of the pet owning population ranges from "user" based dogma, where an animal is allotted no sentient capabilities and maintained strictly for the benefit of the owner; to those who hold animals as dear and precious as a human member of the family. As with most things, where we humans can tend to take extreme views, finding balance in our perspectives and providing for the animal's needs in a way they can appreciate can have reciprocal benefits that enhance the over-all relationship. Social animal needs are similar across the range of domestic and wild species as are the consequences of those needs not being met.

Though domestic dog's thought processes and maturity are limited, they're vulnerable to many of the same psychological challenges we see in humans today. Veterinary medicine now includes treatment for: mental health based symptoms, separation anxiety, reactivity, and obsessive compulsive behaviours. If we hold these trends up to humans' statistics, it's clear that vets have had to include treatment for psychiatric diseases to assuage pet owner's anxieties, that have been subconsciously projected onto their pets.

Those phone company commercials, where the dogs and owners look like each other, are accurate, but not by appearance, so much as by personality.

A police officer once related that as a "rule of thumb," if there was a dog in the front yard of a house, you could tell 'what' was behind the door, from how the dog behaved.

A good friend and veterinarian, who practises both Western and Eastern philosophy medicine, went further by saying that people will often bring in apparently healthy dogs. When at a loss in finding physical symptoms, she inevitably asks the client, "So how have you been feeling?" The majority of clients then go on to mirror, with subtly different adjectives, the same disease symptoms, they have brought their dog in for her to treat.

The potential for psychological disorders in social species animals is possible, but given the structure of their brains compared to our own, they are not as prone to mental health issues as us big-brained critters. Their inability to maintain self-awareness is their best defence. Without it, they are incapable of spending hours, days, or even months feeling sorry for themselves.

Studies have shown social species animals can be coerced into developing addictive "personalities". However, compared to their human counterparts, the depth and degree of their addictions are not usually as severe or destructive.

To review their similarities: Domestic animals differ, in subtle ways, from their wild counterparts. In most cases, size, shape, and physical ability are much the same. Mentally, they are capable of similar degrees of language, etiquette, and hierarchy, though with less 'wisdom' with which to carry out their instinctual drives.

Instinctually, our domestic animals retain most of the subconscious patterns present in their wild counterparts. We see this when dogs spin around before lying down, and in their greeting behaviours of submissive licking around the mouth. Their instinctual drives have been retained and, in some breeds, specifically highlighted for human service: border collies, retrievers, German shepherds. Most working dog breeds present their inherited "compulsions" with very little human input or training.

Nonverbal language skills, like posturing and facial expressions, are all present in one immature form or another. They span the entire family of canine species regardless of, domestic or wild heritage, geological placement, or diet.

Our domestic canines have similar physical capacities to their wild relatives, but lack the mental maturity.

Few clients jump up and down cheering when told that, simply put, domestication equals retardation of mental maturity. Our quasi-wolves are permanent dunderheads, when compared to their big cousins.

In order to keep my audience, I have to be quick in explaining the benefits of this mass "retardation" program.

The benefits to inhibited maturity are many. Like old Ben, they can retain, throughout a long life, the carefree joie de vivre present only for a short time in youthful, wild social species. Presumably, before life's stresses take most of the carefree spark out and replace it with defensive, protection, postures and behaviours.

Another benefit of domestication is the malleability of domesticated animals. Rather than having their fears and compulsions highlighted by experience, and the wisdom prevalent and accrued in wild canines, our dogs remain open to being manipulated into accepting foreign environments and situations, including people and different species, at the drop of a hat, at any age.

By way of example a one year old zebra colt, would fight to exhaustion if captured and roped like a 'wild' horse (wild horses are more accurately defined as feral). It would be a dangerous goal to attempt, let alone hope to succeed, in training the wild animal at that stage of mental development.

A domestic horse, even a wild born and bred version, captured at a year, would present a far different picture. Handled properly, within an hour the animal could be convinced to, not only accept but, take comfort from the touch of the same man who had just ended its life of freedom.

Our dog's malleability comes from that retarded maturity level. As infants, most species are programmed to take information in, and use that information to develop neurological patterns that will assist in its survival within the environment it's raised.

Our dogs, incapable of forming mature perspectives, are destined to repeat their most recent successfully learned behaviours. Once they reach domestication's version of mental maturity, they are figuratively at the end of the line for developmental changes, insights, and cognitive abilities. Our dogs, no matter how large or small in stature, will go through life portraying infantile, adolescent wolf-like behaviour. Their instincts may compel them to attempt half-hearted challenges for leadership, seen in everyday life as 'misbehaviour'. But, in reality, it's the adolescent mind trying to make sense of ancient patterns, rising up as instincts that lead our dogs to 'play' at being a grown-up.

If left unchecked in a way that the pup can understand, another 'fantasy' may take shape, increasing the dog's challenges. We should view these events as, the animal trying to decipher "*What the hell is really going on*" in its environment, compared to what the dog instinctually knows should be its 'reality'. If we can understand this view that our dogs have, we can prepare ourselves to provide for them, in a way in which they need learn nothing more than what they are "born knowing," and what they have already picked up, in their first 6 or 8 weeks of life, with their mother and the social environment their litter provided for them.

We can reinforce their instinctual perspectives, comforting them through our <u>imitations</u> of their mother's actions, expressions, and language. We can teach humans a simple language that can be used on their waiting pets offering, in most cases, instant benefits and rewards for both species involved. What we are looking to create is a relationship with our animals. Relationships, and their success or failure, depend on just a few key elements: trust, understanding, and communication.

In the next sections, we will look at how to develop trust, increase understanding based on this 'muted' wolf perspective, and lastly, develop communication strategies that will bridge the gap, between our two species, in a simple and naturally occurring way.

For further suggested reading on the above topic check out authors such as Desmond Morris (Dog Watching, 1986) or Konrad Lorenz 1973, nobel prize winner, acclaimed as one of the founders of Ethology (Man Meets Dog, 1950).

Breed Anomalies

The effects of selective breeding have resulted in some outrageous and amazing creatures. On one extreme we've created the Border Collie.

The Border Collie is a canine that, through language skills and behaviour, demonstrates an exceptional amount of reasoning ability and memory. In many instances, they have demonstrated decision making skills that surpass other domestic dogs. Their potential indicates an advanced measure of maturity when compared to other domestic breeds. Border Collies' ability to effectively "Herd", in a multiple dog cooperative, is only out-done by the skills of their wild counterparts. To compare a group of Poodles or German Shepherds doing the same job, we'd immediately appreciate the difference in fluidity and group cohesiveness.

A Border Collie will herd, no matter what its upbringing. They'll herd anything: remote control cars, humans, or water from the end of a hose. It's rare, when one is born that doesn't have an inclination toward herding <u>something</u>.

The point behind all this Border Collie hoopla, is that the black and white, or tri-coloured dog that we know today, has only been specifically bred for a little over a 150 years!

If we look at their compulsions to herd, after just a century and a half of selective breeding, we should ask ourselves, "How deep do the compulsions run in dogs that have been bred selectively for hundreds or thousands of years?"

Should we be more surprised when a Border Collie, raised in downtown Vancouver, performs a perfect Fetch the first time it's brought in to see livestock? Or if the "Butcher's Dog" the Rottweiler, has a tendency to bite and hold anytime the 'butcher' is perceived, by the dog, to be in need of back up?

With the myriad of breeds and mixes of dogs present on earth, it's difficult to get a true breed history. Many breeds are new blends of popular old ones: designer dogs - Labradoodles, Malti-poos, or Pugles...For Dog's sake!

To get a head start on knowing what our dogs will be like, understanding the original 'function' the breed was designed to fill, is very important.

Not many of us, these days, have the 'need' for a dog that was designed to live in thirty below zero weather, pull heavy loads for dozens of miles, and then fight polar bears at night. That's not meant to be a disparaging remark about northern breed dogs - it's meant to focus on the truth of how important it is to be 'kind' to an animal's nature. Not all dogs are meant for 'Doing the Dog Park'.

To check our breed's history, we need to dig beyond the glossy magazines produced by breeders and kennel clubs. History is rarely shiny or cute. Usually, it's dusty and full of many reasons why things are the way they are today.

When we visualize back into our shared pasts, the origins and purposes of our different dog breeds take on a more intimate feel. If we imagine ourselves, tens of thousands of years ago, at the edge of an ancient glacier, by today's standards, we'd possess pretty much nothing: a few skins, furs for warmth, special pointy sticks, and some cool rocks we'd knocked together to make sharp tools. Wolves were drawn to our kills and garbage piles, and would have acclimated to our presence. These curious wolves would have been the source of our first companion animals.

What jobs would we have had for them that would have justified the development of our mutually beneficial relationships? Enter the age and development of hunting dogs. Naturally co-operative hunters, they'd have corralled or steered fleeing herds back toward their slower, two-legged associates, who could then finish the hunt. The wolf-dog's social instincts would also have brought them to high regard, for alerting and defending territories from other predators.

From that point on, as we've progressed through our civilizations' growth, dogs have been with us every step of the way. Selective breeding developed dogs suited for human service, based on their predecessor's size, looks, and natural talents. From draft dogs capable of pulling nearly a ton, to little tea-cup canines, created solely for human companionship, each breed and blend we have today, can trace its roots to those wild buggers that got into our ancestors garbage.

Some anomalies in dog behaviour, are attributable to breed origin, and the jobs they were created to do for a living.

Of our modern dogs, the ancient guardian dog lines seem to have suffered most of all, in terms of susceptibility to neurological distress. Their original job: to hang out with a bunch of grass eaters and "Remove any threat," seems to have dictated that they be selectively bred to be low input, low output, devises.

In other words, their forefathers needed to be happy watching the grass grow, but still be capable of occasional bouts of herd protecting. Today, if we amp up their input with over-stimulation, travel, fatigue, or too much change, we can see some really off-the-wall behaviours and fears develop. Including: sensitivities to sights and sounds, object aversions, declines in confidence levels, and emotional instability. In their 'natural place' guardian dogs are some of the most stable and dependable breeds. Their limited _IQ's_ can predispose them to the adverse effects of stress when they are overwhelmed with too much information.

Being aware of our dog's 'history' will help us predict which skills our dogs will most naturally express. If we're avid cross country ski enthusiasts, a chihuahua or greyhound might have a hard time enjoying the deep powder, as much as we do. Or, if we spend winter months in equatorial heat, our malamutes might melt trying to keep cool by pool.

CHAPTER TWO
The Truth About Rules

As the session moves on, we'll start talking about the cause of their problems. With a clearer perspective of their young-minded animal's world, some clients jump to the right conclusion without being prompted. Some start to see how those common, often innocuous behaviours present in our dogs, are really just the animal's way of seeking fulfillment for innate social needs, that were programmed into their little heads and hearts long, before they were ever born. Some dogs, especially those with human or dog aggression problems, appear too malevolent for such a simple solution to make immediate sense.

Ryder

Ryder was a year and a half old, long, leggy, shepherd who showed up with his people, a young professional couple, Leigh and Georgette. They carried the look of a worried pair, after incidents involving aggression toward humans and other dogs.

When they arrived, I had them leave the dog in the car while they gave me some back ground information. We talked for a bit. After they'd given me a clearer picture of what I'd seen behind the windshield in their car, I asked them to bring Ryder out, and attach him to a rope anchored near where we had been sitting on the patio. While they fetched their dog, I went inside to get another chair, and a left-over chicken breast I had in the fridge.

I had set up the place where the dog would be tied, so that he could *almost* reach the spot where I would sit. The couple would share a bench, on the same side of the table as their dog, and I'd be at the head of the table, closest to the dog, but off to the side.

Poor Ryder's first face-to-face glimpse of me was as a head, appearing over this hovering chair that I carried out of the house, just as his people sat down. The chair, floating above the table, spooked him bad enough, but when he saw my face appear as I set it down, I was a marked man in his eyes. He barked and growled, while he swung like a pendulum on the end of his leash, moving as close to his people as he could, then as far away from all of us as possible. The growls ended in a higher pitched sound, almost a whine. He was very uneasy.

I sat with my body positioned about 3/4's of a turn away from him. He could see my back and part of my face. I ignored him completely, after sitting down, and we continued our talk about where the dog had come from, and how their problems had come about. Ryder settled, after a few minutes and lay down, with all four legs under him, about fifteen feet from the table. He lay down, but was still alert, and would watch me closely, with every move I made. He'd decided he didn't like me.

After one or two of their earliest incidents, they'd signed up for a dog training class, in their community, called a 'Growl' class. I live about an hour from where they live, and had heard someone had started teaching a class by that title. I thought it was great! I'd been teaching people to *growl* for years, and sometimes felt self-conscious, and a little 'out-there'. When they mentioned that they'd gone, I asked them to show me how they were taught to growl.

"Well, we didn't actually growl, that's just what they called the class," Georgette replied. Georgette was a high school teacher, who looked like she was hardly old enough to be out of school, let alone teaching hard-assed teenagers to toe the line. Her husband Leigh, a good natured, calm, quiet, young guy, nodded his agreement. He had a sparkle of mischief in his eyes, so I think he figured something was up, when I'd been tickled about their growl class.

"That's okay. I'll teach you how to growl", I offered.

Ryder was acclimating to my presence, but far from at ease. I continued to ignore him, and began the session with the picture of the Christmas tree and the regular spiel. It didn't take them long to realize how Ryder's problems originated from two separate areas.

First, the personality that he was born with was one prone to being a worrier. He had confidence, borne of his size and the environment Leigh and Georgette had created for him, but his innate anxiety levels could get the better of him, at times of stress or exhaustion.

The second contributing factor to his problems, stemmed from his skewed perspective that had grown, over time, by slight mistakes in care and handling. Like many owners, their mistakes had been made with the best intentions. Through Ryder's eyes, the love and caring they showered on him didn't equate to competent leaders, who could fend off an attack from... the rottie across the street, or that scary dude who showed up every day, when they weren't home, and put paper in the tin box outside the door. Ryder's, immature, but intelligent, mind *knew* there needed to be a strong figure in the household, but Leigh and Georgette's strengths weren't visible to the dog's limited scope of understanding.

Leigh was average height, in good physical shape, calm, and exuded a good-natured confidence. Georgette was slim, with an outgoing attitude. Both were intelligent, energetic, successful, young adults, at a loss for what to do with their dog's antisocial behaviour.

Ryder stayed alert to our conversation interrupting, from time to time, with a quiet whine. He would stand occasionally, and pace in short sweeps over the area that he had decided was a safe distance from the "chair-guy."

He watched me closely whenever I spoke loud, or made fast gestures. He really didn't know what to make of me. He'd never been around a person who totally ignored him, yet separated him from his people. His initial impression of me, with the chair held up in front of my body, walking toward him, even when he'd tried to warn me away, was one of complete uncertainty. He couldn't read what he had come to expect from people in my demeanour. I wasn't showing signs of being scared of him. I was neutral toward him, yet as I spoke to his people, I was animated, at times loud, and through the material I covered, I would wind-up showing examples of emotional expressions and body postures. Ryder could see, from where he was that I was confident, that I had emotions, and I expressed myself clearly. He had stopped growling at me after a few minutes, and I could see he was trying to get comfortable in this foreign situation.

Finally, the time came to talk about how the Momma wolf says no, and how ownership is her 'god given right'. Unlike Porter, Ryder had not been physically dominated into insincere submission. His aggression was a symptom of his anxiety and uncertainty. He didn't know whose role was whose. Being able to differentiate between the myriad of aggression causes, and undertaking to resolve them, should never be entered into lightly. An animal's life hangs in the balance, as well as potential external damage it may inflict, while in an aggressive state. Ryder's 'type' of aggression was the kind that is easy to remedy, and if handled appropriately, and in a timely manner, can be resolved permanently.

* * *

In a teasing voice, I asked them again, "So you didn't actually growl in your growl class?"

They shook their heads and watched, as I picked up the chicken breast I'd put on the table at the beginning of the session. I still hadn't looked directly at Ryder, since sitting down. I used my peripheral vision to figure out the best place to toss the chicken. It landed just inside the dog's reach, about three feet from my chair. I kept my eyes on Leigh and Georgette, watching the dog from the corner of my eye. He approached the chicken faster than I thought he would, and I reacted accordingly. When his nose was about a foot and a half from the treat, I *exploded* in my chair. Still seated, I spun around to square off over the chicken. My upper body loomed toward the dog. My right hand shot out toward him, fingers splayed and curled, like imitation teeth warning the dog away from *my food*. I snarled, and growled a low-toned possessive warning, my eyes drilled into his - daring him to remain where he was.

These actions had three different effects on my audience. Within a 1/2 second, Ryder, shocked at hearing his own language for the first time from a human, retreated with haste as far as his leash would allow. Georgette looked like she was going to cry. Leigh, after his initial surprise, looked like a little boy who'd been turned loose in a toy store.

I was able to watch the human reaction, because Ryder's had been so honest and fast. He'd understood that chicken wasn't his, in an instant, and had retreated. In the instant he started moving backward, I turned back to my normal position and ignored him.

"That's how a momma says "No."" I smiled.

Georgette was the most affected of the bunch. The shock of what I'd done was so unexpected, she was like Ryder had been, watching me with suspicion, anxious at what my next weird move would be. By the time everyone's heart rate was back to normal, I brought their attention to Ryder. He had come back from where he had been. Instead of the nervousness and suspicion he was lying down. Relaxed, with all four legs spread out to the side, about four feet from where I was, his feet almost to the imaginary line he had crossed with his nose when I had growled at him. I reached down, pulled a piece of meat off the chicken breast and tossed it to Ryder, who caught and ate it. The next piece I fed him by hand. I got up and unhooked him from the fence. We went for a walk, while his people watched from the table.

While we walked, Ryder relaxed a bit more and became more trusting of who I was. He wasn't enamoured with me, but he respected me enough, after our discussion about who's chicken it was, that he was no longer of the mind to act aggressively toward me. He engaged in some light rough-housing with me, but he was not a dog to trust and relax quickly, so it was perfunctory and stiff on his part. He played with me because he knew I wanted him to. Because I owned the chicken, and had shared it with him, he figured that I wasn't such a bad guy after all.

The irony in the above story is how Ryder's stance

toward me was changed. Most people are encouraged to 'ease' into a relationship with a dog. This is sound advice. If there is one golden rule of dogs, it is: Always let them come to you. Ryder came to me, or rather, the chicken. I spoke his language, with a firm and clear voice. Initially it surprised him, but after he had had a moment to process what had gone on, he felt more at ease and accepting of me than he had before. He understood my claim to the food, and how I reacted after his retreat.

The best way to understand our dog's state of mind is to acknowledge their muted-wolf background, and how it holds them in an immature state. Ryder was the size of a wolf, but his mind was, is, and always will be, locked at the point of maturity where he can only guess at how to use his instincts. Leigh and Georgette, up to that point, had not given him clear indications of who led or what was appropriate, and he had been trying to figure out for himself how his world worked.

Leigh and Georgette went on to understand and provide for Ryder in such a way, that he no longer felt compelled to act aggressively toward strangers and new dogs. They know he'll be prone to relapses, brought on by stress or fatigue, but through clear communication and empathy, they can safely and predictably enjoy their dog on social occasions, or in novel environments, without fear of him going goofy again.

For the purposes of this section, we will concern ourselves with our domestic canine's fundamental needs. How we can provide for them and how, by doing so, we will reduce liability, and stress, improve health, and help create a more enriched and secure environment for those we care for.

Our dogs' suppressed maturity levels make it important to note that they cannot fully appreciate or perceive the intricacies of an alpha led hierarchy. The subtleties of language and social politics are beyond their full grasp. Yet, they still retain those instinctual motivators, muted but still based in acquiring comfort for their innate survival and social needs.

In order to make the best of the above truths, we'll need to appreciate what it is they can be fully aware of, or to what depth they truly understand their emotions and environments.

Let's start with their view of relationships. To do that, let's return to what we know about their wild counterparts.

Infant wild canines spend their time sleeping with, wrestling with, or grooming litter-mates. Like watching a gaggle of kids in a daycare centre, their free time is play-oriented, with bouts of exploration. Most adult members of the pack avoid them like the plague. Their main point of reference is their mother. She is the be-all and end-all for them. She provides their food, discipline, and nurturing, as well as honing their early behavioural responses and burgeoning skills.

Her tender ministrations in still healthy brain

development that creates the foundation for later adult stability. Her interactions with them, surrounding play, feeding, or exploration, highlight natural instincts toward hunting, social behaviours, language development, and safety.

In their natural state, from birth until adolescence, canine pups exist in the periphery of the society they will one day join. Socializing and growing up, within a micro-version of their future reality. These 12 - 16 weeks of relative seclusion, allow the pups to develop and grow, both in size and mental capacity, at a rate that's suited to their development. Their observation skills develop early. From their position on the periphery, they can watch in relative safety, the goings-on of the older juveniles, their squabbles and solutions. They start to see the levels within the queen's court.

Then, much like children emulating adult behaviour, they have a "tea-party". Instead of tables and chairs, cups and saucers, canine tea-parties include activities, like stalking, bullying, feigning body postures, trying on facial expressions, teasing, and of course, wrestling.

We can't know how they come to their decisions to play whatever roles they chose. But we can observe their actions, compare them to those of adults in their day to day lives, and then draw conclusions that, social and survival skills development is motivated by the pup's instincts, wants, and needs. If we watch how pups play, they are first drawn to stalking: a bug crawling over their paw - then pursuit! Their games grow in degrees. Similar to how a human infant's games progress from simple to more complex. As they get older, more involved games of pursuit with other litter-mates, advance to wrestling matches with older juvenile animals.

We can be sure they don't have the fore-thought or language skills that our children do, in creating elaborate set-ups and themes. But the pups get their ideas from somewhere - instinctual drives. In whatever way they acquire these ideas, their games further refine skills and abilities, that will become necessary for them to succeed in their future 'world order'.

We can modify instinctual drives but, like their personalities, they will always be a part of them. An example of an instinctual drive would be the scenario of a domestic orphaned pup we raised. Bottle fed from birth, and *denned* up at night in a travel cage, the pup quickly adapted to sleeping through the night without waking.

In nature, from birth until around 3 1/2 weeks, the pups are den-bound and make only minor excursions outside their dim lit safe place. The mother will clean the den of excrement by re-ingesting the waste produced by her pups. At that age they exist solely on her milk. All of that changes the day they start eating solid foods. The pups are then required to do their business outside. For years I thought that this behaviour was due to maternal influence. This orphan changed my belief.

He was a peaceful little guy, well-adjusted and much loved by my four, then small children. He would sleep through the night from a surprisingly early age. At 3 weeks old he was introduced to his first taste of real food. At 3:00am the same night, he woke me up with urgent cries and scratching. He wanted out of his crate. He waddled a couple steps and had his first Food Propelled bowel movement! Then, that was it. Half-asleep, he turned around and went back to bed. I cleaned up the first of his stinky messes and sat smiling over what he'd shown me. Instinctual drives are cool!

Domestic and wild pups depend on their mother for all their needs, both physical and emotional. This dependency remains intact, in both versions, until late puberty.

Our domestic dogs' mental maturity ceases to develop around the stage where the wild pups are just being incorporated into the "real world" of canine society. In that light, they obtain a good deal of dependency, bold enough to interact with others, brave enough to venture out on their own, strong enough to play and hunt. But they still need mom to tuck them in at night

For our purposes, this point begins to define those needs inherent in our dogs for their whole life. If we can acknowledge and understand how those needs work, how they affect the animal's development and behaviour, we have the opportunity to create an environment that is richer, with fewer constraints, less stress, and markedly more rewarding. Defining their needs, in this light, will guide us to a clearer picture of our own responsibilities, and the course of actions we can take to provide for their innate needs.

Richard A. Wolters speculated, in his 1964 book <u>Water Dog</u>, that a pup's mind at 7 weeks, was ready to learn anything it will ever need to learn, and that the pup was only limited by its physical abilities. His opinion struck a chord, and through the years, I've come to believe in it. A pup's early capacity for learning can be staggering.

I was challenged by a movie script, one time, to provide a small pup that could fit in a purse, appear as a young pup, and yet perform the behaviours called for in the script. They wanted the 'image' of a six week old orphan. The window of opportunity for finding, training, and then shooting with a young pup is small. I found two candidates to act as doubles for each other. They were 3 1/2 week old Border collie pups. Training began while they were still with their mother. By 5 1/2 weeks, they were in front of the cameras doing more than I had ever thought possible. Between the two pups, we had taught them all their obedience commands as well as: to crawl (out from under a blanket), fetch, speak, and put their head down to feign sleep. We had also taught them to stand up and scratch at a door, to be let out of the dreaded shelter kennel.

They have the mental capacity to do so much, at such a young age, yet they are destined to live out their lives in a mental 'Peter-Pan' state. That's a good thing for us! And not so bad for them either.

It's a good thing because, in their immature state, we

can predict their needs and provide for them in such a way as to create a relationship based on the dog's level of perception and natural understanding, leading to a harmonious Mother-child hierarchy.

Basic survival-needs span all animal life forms: food, water, shelter. These basic needs are just the foundation for a much more involved list of social species needs that include companionship, sense of security, privacy, and status. These innate needs are crucial to recognize. For now, acknowledging their existence, and utility in relationship building with our pets, is sufficient.

With this list in front of us, we turn to acquisition. Acknowledging how we acquire sustenance for our own needs is a start. We can then transfer that understanding to juvenile, then infant human acquisition techniques. This gives us a place of understanding that we can then, without anthropomorphizing, relate to our domestic canines behaviours and how they are linked to their innate needs.

It's usually our dog's acquisition techniques that create human animosity. Behaviours like whining, jumping up on people, barking, uninvited contact, etc., come from the dog's own language/society. In their world it's how they 'get things.' This perspective covers most unwanted behaviours like an umbrella. If we can provide for our dogs, in a way that takes care of their physical and emotional needs, then we've solved a good majority of 'dog problems' in one fell swoop.

* * *

The way to get from here to there is a short, straight line. If we can implement one rule, that has two parts, we will have solved the vast majority of dog/human challenges.

One rule, two parts

We began by identifying the types of needs our dogs have. If we take a minimalist view of their needs, and cover those basic physical and emotional necessities from what we have at hand, it's easier to accept the simplistic solution we are about to discuss, compared to the "hurry up and do something" philosophies currently in practise, surrounding training and behaviour modification.

A 'dependant being' is essentially motivated by fears. Fear of injury, of hunger, of thirst, of isolation, and on and on it can go. These fears, real or imagined, motivate the individual to behave in any way that minimizes the chances of their fears being realized. In that way, our dogs are motivated, subconsciously, to perform behaviours that we humans often describe as "he's trying to please me." In his way, he is. He wants to please you, but for his own reasons. So that those instinctual fears he carries don't come true! In his puppy-mind, he needs you to feed him, caress him, protect him, give him water, and entertainment. That's all those necessities his mother provided for him, when he was a baby. In his mind, these needs, once fulfilled, equate to a sense of wellbeing. We can relate it to the "après" feast feeling around a Thanksgiving Day table. An immature mind is programmed to seek comfort and reward continually. It's difficult to remember this when living with a creature that can develop from a cute cuddly infant, to a terrorizing miniature version of its adult self, in just a few short weeks.

The simplest way for us to provide for their needs, is by imitating the behaviour of their own mother. Taking on the Mother role, we reduce those fears and provide sensory proof to the pup that "all is as it should be." In being "who" the dog needs us to be, we do away with much of the frustration and distress that can grow through improper perspectives. The role we take can make teaching the dog a far more pleasant experience, reducing negative experiences and associations that can be accumulated by harsh training practises or unfulfilled needs. Like Ryder, many dogs, destined for difficult times, can have a world opened up to them in the blink of an eye. Their life-long immature state provides hope for even adult or senior animal perspective change. They just need to "See" the right figurehead in their lives.

To become the figurehead our dogs can naturally and cognitively relate to, we must become (in their eyes), their surrogate Mother. The only other figure or position that is understandable to them [at their mental maturity level] is their litter-mates.

Anyone who has raised a litter of pups a full 12 weeks knows that you don't want to be seen as just another pup in the pile! Think: "Lord Of The Flies", with teeth and claws.

This train of thought becomes the 'Rule'. One simple

rule with two parts:

1. Be The Mom

We can "Be the Mom" by exemplifying Part A and Part B of the rule, and by using language skills that are native to the species with which we work. A real canine mother is the light of her pups' lives. She provides sustenance, nurturing, and discipline, across the activities and learning opportunities the developing pups' experience. She provides for their emotional needs, as well as all their physical needs. She's the Giver and Taker-away of the Warm-n-Fuzzies.

Rule One: Part A - Own Everything

Owning "Everything" is not a new mantra to dog trainers. What should be new here, are the degrees that "Everything" entails. Some training manuals, veterinary advice, and trainers will quickly outline the most tangible items on this list. Things like: food, toys, beds, furniture. Anything real, physical, objects you can taste, touch or see.

Of equal importance of '*things to own*,' are those items that are intangible: contact, space, quiet, affection, and even play. The world is full of intangible 'things' to own. Each dog is as different from each other as we are and they can find unique ways to perceive environments or scenarios, that can lead to 'assumptions' of ownership, privilege, or rights.

Owning everything tangible and intangible, is the most profound way in which we can demonstrate, to our dogs, that we are capable and that we understand them, will care for them, and can be trusted to do so - no matter what life throws our way.

This is a foreign concept to most people's way of thinking. None of us want to be confined, controlled or denied. We strive for freedom, and naturally assume those same desires belong to our animals. Piles of toys, food, and beds adorn the floors of most pet owner's homes. We want our animals to have everything they need, and we lavish them with all we can provide. Unfortunately, dogs weigh and measure individuals and their 'position', based on their observations and interactions.

People coming home from a long day at work and squealing "Hello", while they excitedly greet their frantic pups, accomplish two things: one that they intend and one that they don't. The dog sees and feels the "love". But, it also sees Mom acting like a Pup! The pup's real mom came home from the hunt with sore feet and a tired back. Not one pup in the litter would dare tumble her over in a vigorous greeting, until she said it was time. She would say when it was time for the greeting, and who would be greeted first.

In their immature state of mind they will be curious of, and test perpetually. If a mother fails to provide for her pups, or falls short of the mark, she can expect the pup or pups to test her resolve and abilities, to make sure she's not just a big litter-mate! They do the same to us when we fail to depict that Big Momma image.

The canine mother, conscious of this or not, uses Part B of the only rule, to minimize the instinctual testing her pups will do.

One Rule, Part B - Start and Stop Everything

When Momma owns everything, it's a simple matter for her to instruct her young on when they can do something, or when they cannot.

Their understanding is that mom owns everything. Anything they have, tangible or intangible, is on loan from her. She initiates this before their eyes are open. When the pups nurse, she lies still and allows them to feed. When she feels they've had enough, or she's compelled to leave, she simply removes the food supply - without apology or excuses. "It is what it is." A like it, or lump it kinda thing. They learn early on that whining about it doesn't help. As they develop, she initiates and dictates the start and end of grooming, play, or quiet times. She ends conflicts and starts new activities, without leaving the pups any doubts or questions.

Advice, from Veterinarians and trainers, that tell people to ensure they can 'play' with their dog's food, or take it away while the dog is eating, are trying to get this point across.

In the wild, a pup that happened to jerk the hind leg off a deer and drag it away from the group to eat it, wouldn't think to argue when Mom came over and wanted it. If it could, it would say something like: "Oh! You want this? Here ya' go! Can I get you a drink of water with that?"

Mom wouldn't have to growl or threaten to persuade the pup to relinquish the food. Her proximity, and a look from her, would do it. Her ownership is already implied. All that was needed from her was the 'word,' ...which leads us to the most important skill we all have and use to acquire what we want.

Language.

CHAPTER THREE

The Truth About Language

Language

After making the rules clear, most clients are eager to get on with the session and find out how to start implementing them. Communication skills are what we need to do it.

Language is essential to all life forms. An electrical charge between synapses can be a rudimentary form of communication, a spark of energy triggering one organ to tell another "Now!" It can be simple or complex, with multi-layered meanings or innuendo. Language can be seen everywhere we turn, from the flight patterns of birds, to a marching line of ants hauling goodies home from a picnic blanket.

How we interpret language and express ourselves determines how aware and fluent we can be in relation to others. In human-dog relationships, we should first focus on teaching the more <u>intelligent</u> animal new perspectives and communication skills. This is a faster, more effective way to enjoy our canine companions, and it reduces the pressures on them to learn new skills. This focus also helps minimize stress and liability, for those dogs that have fear or aggression problems.

In this section, we'll highlight the principals of effective communication between man and dog. It's the make-or-break point for many. Without communication skills, it doesn't matter how much you love something and want things to work out. If we can't effectively communicate our wants, needs, or desires, it's likely that the relationship will be unfulfilling or lacking.

We have the ability to communicate on multiple levels, at one time. Scientists, like Paul Eckman, have spent their careers identifying and documenting the different forms of communication we use: facial expressions, eye contact, body posture, and gait. The list goes on and on. Many people are surprised by how little communication has to do with verbal speech or dialect.

We'll dissect our own forms of communicating first, turn to the many similarities we share with other social animals, and then identify the few differences.

Layers of Language

If we were suddenly unable to speak, we would still be able to communicate. We'd find ways to acquire those things we need to fulfil our social, physical, and emotional needs.

Language enables us to share our ideas, emotions, thoughts, and needs. Human language has been broken down into verbal and nonverbal parts. For an animal that is as verbose as we are, the division is startling. The majority of studies rate nonverbal language components at between 60 - 80% of our conversations' content. Only 20 – 40% is allocated to our words.

We rely heavily on our auditory senses for sharing ideas and thoughts. But when it comes to expressing our emotions, it seems they were made to be worn on our sleeve. To find adequate <u>words</u> to communicate the experience of our feelings is usually a disappointing task. But, when we add facial expressions, tone, and body language, the audience experiences the full effect of the speaker's gist.

To clarify: our verbal skills only provide the basis for our discussions, a black and white sketch. Our other senses fill the picture with colour. Our eyes garner information that indicates a person's approachability, demeanour, rough age, and sometimes, even their intents. Our ears tell us the significance of their tone, giving us details about their emotional state. Our sense of smell lets us know if someone has washed or not, smell healthy or sick, scared or aroused. Touch is one of our most heightened senses, yet is one of the most subjective that we have. Our largest organ, skin, is a vast sensory unit tuned to temperature, humidity, pressure, and texture. The touch of a mother or a lover can have similar mechanical functions, yet the emotions shared are markedly different. Taste is integrally linked to the other senses. It's capable of basic taste sensations, but also able to stimulate perceptions effecting our emotions and memories, as well as physiological changes in saliva and gut acid production.

The senses we have are responsible for collecting the full colour we enjoy from communicating. The brain is able to process combinations of stimuli, and create full colour conclusions to the myriad of possible meanings from a speaker. Like any other skill, the more we practise the better we become.

With our senses in check - let's look at how our body communicates nonverbally.

The following overview of nonverbal expression components, are the most commonly used and easily identifiable. It's important to note that, to include a detailed discussion and deciphering of all forms of human nonverbal communication is both beyond my abilities and our needs, for the purposes of this work. It is a fascinating field, and I encourage anyone who is interested, to explore the topic more deeply through the many online volumes dedicated to its study, or published works by such renowned authors as Paul Eckman and Desmond Morris. The subject is fascinating and ever evolving, giving deeper meaning and insights into our own psyches, as well as those of the animals around us.

Eyes

"<u>The eyes are the windows to the soul</u>" - Old English proverb.

This saying is as true today as at any time in our past. Not only are they the proverbial windows, but they're also a darn good 'lighthouse' in telegraphing what's going on in the emotional part of the brain. As a nonverbal communication device, they aren't just the round, fluid filled orbs that are our literal eyes, but include: how the eye is used, in conjunction with the eyelids and eyebrows, as well as the other facial features that are involved as part of the full facial expression. They also possess one facet of expression that we cannot control, the dilation of our pupils. Pupils dilate from extremes in emotion: fear, sexual arousal, surprise, and anger. Eyes, or rather eye contact, have the ability to apply an almost physical pressure, even from across a room.

In most social mammals, direct eye contact is considered a challenge. There are amorous exceptions, of course. Why then do we teach our children to 'look someone in the eye' when they are talking with them? We do it because that's how we were taught, or our parents incorrectly passed on what they'd been taught. Instead, we should teach our children to look at the person's face while speaking with them. The difference to the receiver is immense! A soft gaze, floating from one feature to another and then back again, making appropriate stops to check in with the other's eyes, is comfortable and un-intrusive. But, when someone does 'Look us in the eye" while they are talking, and doesn't look away, I don't care who you are, how big or how small the other is - it's intimidating, unsettling, exciting, or distracting. It all depends on the source and its intent. All the great apes are the same way, and the trait runs heavily through all social species mammals.

Facial expressions

From wrinkled brow to beaming smiles, faces are our mind's billboard. Most of our facial expressions are produced without us being conscious of them. How many times have we been busy with our own thoughts, when someone comments on how we 'appear' – "My, don't you look happy today!" or "Hey buddy, why so glum?"

The tilt of our head, tension of facial muscles, set of our jaws, or flaring of our nostrils - all fit together as an announcement of what's going on inside, and how we're feeling about what is going on around us. Another old English adage fits here, "Chin up!" The higher up one's chin is, the more confident that person would have people believe they are feeling. A scientific theory was recently put forward that hopes to prove that, 'acting' a certain way is likely to promote the emotions that accompany the posture.

Some societies are raised from birth to maintain a deadpan outward appearance. Not so much Caucasians of European descent: those emotional-fiery Celts sowed a lot of genetic traits! But many North American First Nations and Asiatic cultures are raised with unspoken societal codes that promote minimal use of facial expressions. In spite of societal conditioning, repressing facial expressions takes conscious effort.

I mentioned Paul Eckman earlier. His research surrounding facial expressions has revolutionized many fields of study: forensic interviewing, counselling, psychiatry, human resource development, and on and on. His work has benefited any field that relies on discovering true emotions in human communications, particularly where the subject is prone to lie. One of his most exciting discoveries is what he called Micro-expressions.

He travelled the world and showed photographs of people's faces expressing different emotions. He found seven emotions that are represented by facial expressions that supersede spoken words. It didn't matter where in the world you were from, or where the picture was taken; in whatever language the people spoke, they had a name for the emotion. These seven, what I'll call 'base' emotions, are: happy, sad, angry, fear, disgust, contempt, and surprise. Others have gone on to theorize that, the rest of our emotions are derived from blends of two or more of these base emotions that do not have their own specific facial expression, but are expressed as a combination of the emotions they represent.

Micro-expressions, of those seven 'base' emotions, are the antithesis of controlled facial expressions. Lasting as little as a quarter of a second, these minute blasts of pure emotion show up on our faces and are almost impossible to feign or control. Eckman's research and finding, in this branch of science, are precious beyond compare. They bridge cultures, race, age, and time itself, by representing ancient emotions handed down to us from our prehistoric relatives. If we have the opportunity to share space with any of the great apes: chimpanzees, orangutans, or gorillas, and experience their facial expressions in their day to day context, it's not hard to imagine how Neanderthal Man, or Leakey's Lucy (Australopithecus), would have used their facial expressions to get their points across.

Reading human facial expressions and body language is not an exact science. Many influences effect expressions: conscious or unconscious thoughts, environmental situations, or experiences. These add to an individual's perceptions and combine to create their feelings, and ultimately, what their expressions say. We can communicate many different things at the same time - literally mixed emotions.

A person at a pleasant dinner might unconsciously grimace in disgust, if he has a flash-back of a co-worker who was hung over that morning and, say... vomited in the parking lot. The facial expression would be out of context to anyone who noticed it. Because of the likelihood and frequency of these oddball expressions, our brains have developed an area that is specifically tasked with constant monitoring of how we are being perceived by others and vice versa.

Being aware of our 'built-in' ability to read facial

expressions, we can start to transfer that skill-set to other species' nonverbal communications.

A cautionary note: being aware of these, sometimes subtle expressions, and the many influences that can contribute to their manifestation, must be well analyzed before attributing too much weight to decisions based solely on expressions or body language, in both humans and dogs.

Body Posture

Whether it's the eyes, facial expressions, body posture, or muscle tension, one facet can be involved, or all of them at once. Kind of like comparing a huge literary work to its Reader's Digest version. It all depends on what and how the communicator chooses to express themselves. Children, especially those who have not developed the verbal skills to express themselves, provide us with our most unadulterated examples of nonverbal "body-language". Their stomping feet when angry, pouting lips when sad, crossed arms and dropped eyes when "caught," give us a glimpse of their honest emotions.

Like the study of facial expressions in humans, there is a plethora of research and books divining the true meaning of body language. From the tilt of our heads, to the positioning of our arms, legs, hands, or feet - we sometimes give away unconscious clues to our audience that adds to our <u>dialogue</u>.

* * *

To keep it simple and brief, the closer to our bodies we keep our hands and arms, the more 'uneasy' or closed off we are. Crossed arms can mean the person is cold – or that they are 'hugging' themselves in a self-soothing way. Whether cold or self-soothing, the motivation comes from the limbic system, a part of the brain that deals with primal instincts. Those fight or flight, survival mechanisms that are in us all. If you're cold or being made uncomfortable by someone, the unconscious response to the 'threat' is the same, pull in the extremities to conserve heat, or keep them out of the way to avoid being bitten.

What we do with our legs and feet is just as telling. How a person positions themselves in a chair, relative to the door and other people, the placement of their feet, where they focus their gaze in the room, all combine to speak volumes, whereas the words focus only on the ideas and details being shared.

Muscle Tension

Muscle tension, like other nonverbal cues, can be the consequence of one, or many influences being experienced in the mind of the communicator. Our senses collect information that create an emotional response, based on the current situation and past experience - should we be tight muscled, ready for action, or confident and relaxed? Muscle tension is visible in our facial expressions, but can affect the entire body. Someone suffering an anxiety disorder may present with chronic tension that causes neck and shoulder pain, and a host of other symptoms that can surface from head to toe.

Gait

Mammalian locomotion is dependent on skeletal function, supported by muscles, and controlled by neurological direction. These three systems are integrally connected, in this situation. One can't complete the task without the others. Therefore, internal processes (thoughts/emotions) directly affect a person's stride and gait, with very visible results. Who hasn't chuckled while a 40 pound child stomps off to her bedroom, sounding like a herd of elephants?

These same mechanical points of language are applicable when trying to understanding another species' language too. The better we are at reading non-verbal, human language, the better we'll be at deciphering other social species' dialects.

Learning to read another species' body language takes time and practice. Some people have a knack for it and others have to persevere through considerable study or trial and error. A natural way to see improvement in reading a different species *language* is to adapt the philosophy of educators who espouse *immersion* for learning another language.

If we observe a species from a distance, without interfering in their day to day routines, we can start to pick out patterns in their interactions that lead to understanding what is being *said*. Where at first we might just see animals moving around without apparent cause or purpose, facial expressions and body postures emerge to mean something.

It all boils down to our ability to relate body postures and facial expressions with emotions and then to accurately see, from the animal's perspective, the cause of its emotional state. Once the cause of the animal's 'frame of mind' is deduced it's a small step for us to influence what happens next. Being able to control our animal's emotional state eases the challenges of physical control.

When it comes to social species animals, there is another similarity that spans the spectrum. Before putting all the non-verbal and verbal parts together, we need to acknowledge an uncomfortable truth... Everybody Lies.

Deception

"Everybody lies." – Gregory House, House MD sitcom

A retired police officer, turned instructor, opened a week-long "Forensic Interviewing" course with: "Hi, my name is Joe (not his real name) and I'm a liar." He let the nervous giggles die down before continuing. Within a few minutes he had the whole room ruminating about their own uncomfortable truths....

"Everybody lies."

* * *

In a short time, his humour and material had the participants absorbed in the <u>Science</u> of forensic interviewing.

After a synopsis of the coming week he warned the group, "Whatever you do, don't use this at home." And then he laughed, admitting that, in spite of his own advice, he was guilty of using it on his teenaged sons. As the week progressed, the reason for the warning became clear. The name of the class should have been – Interrogation 101. Topics covered the gamut of communication: from written and spoken word, to body posture, facial expression, and physiology. The realization of how deceptive we are, as a species, was unsettling.

Claims have been made that people lie an average of three times during a ten minute conversation. The topic has been examined in numerous books and articles, with no one simple definition accepted, for all degrees or types of deception that are possible. The list is a long one: harmless white lies, lies of omissions, exaggeration, minimization, and on and on it goes. We can't live without them. Many of them start unconsciously, and the debate goes on today regarding the degree of consciousness involved in the initiation of the behaviour. There are strong advocates on the side of conscious, ego-based motivators for lying. At the same time, those advocates can't deny the arguably 'unconscious', lying behaviours in species with lesser cognitive function.

Euclid O. Smith, in his 1987 Cultural Anthropology

article, <u>Deception and Evolutionary Biology</u>, told a story related by H. Kummer (1982), about a juvenile female hamadryas baboon in estrus. She was reported to have mated, with a sub-adult male, by spending twenty minutes edging away from the leader, into a sitting position, where a rock hid her front and arms from him. The leader could see her, but not what she was doing. All that was visible to him was the top of her head and back. In this position, she would groom and then slip behind the rock out of the leader's view and mate with a young male, who had stayed hidden from the dominant male by the rock. Between mating sessions, she would return to where she could peek at the leader, or even approached him and presented herself, after which she would return to the sub-dominant male behind the rock.

Now one has to concede, it's a grand leap of intelligence from baboons to domestic animals, but whether it's an old horse who's learnt to have a sore foot to shorten a work day, or an adult dog jumping up to lick a greeting to the corner of a person's mouth, feigning behaviours, that indicate emotions or needs that are untrue, are everyday parts of social species animal's experience. In that light, no discussion on the nature and dynamics of communication is complete, without wading into the deception dialogue.

The subjectivity of the topic gives rise to an argument that's been going on for decades in our own time, but, more likely, the discussion about deception is as old as our earliest campfires. The argument stems from the definition, or lack thereof, as well as our aversion to the topic. Joe, the instructor mentioned above, is a rarity. His presentation about deception wends its way through the whys and how's of it, to get to the truth in lies.

No one consciously wants to lie. However, stronger compulsions, based in our more primitive brain regions, take the choice away from us, in most cases creating the lie before we're even conscious of it being born. Once underway and in our conscious, our egos would rather *die* than be caught in the act.

For our purposes, let's define deception as: A communication; verbal or nonverbal, that conveys an idea or message to a recipient, that contains information that is contrary to, exaggerated, minimized, or omitted from what the sender believes, and through which the sender is likely to receive a benefit.

Throughout our different relationships with dogs or others, be they human or animal, our ability to detect deception, and how we respond to it, plays a vital role. Not all deceptions are of a malign intent. Many times a lie is used to benefit, both the receiver and the sender, in order to reduce stress from insecure feelings, or to improve their social ties.

"Does this dress make me look fat?"

Our dogs do it too! When they jump up and try to lick the corners of our mouth. In essence they're saying "Momma, feed me, I'm just a baby." When they revert to these behaviours, the dog believes that <u>acting</u> like a pup should result in nurturing responses from its mother. No different than our children reverting to baby-talk. Unfortunately, the dog doesn't realize its muddy paws and sharp nails that mess up the Armani suit foil its best attempts, no matter how convincing it plays at being a baby again.

Every social animal, and many non-social species, depend on deception, from time to time.

Deception, like language is everywhere we look, if not full-out lying, then in milder more *acceptable* forms. The most pervasive assault, that humans face, is the propaganda that berates us daily from ad campaigns, promising we'll be happier if we: Drink this product. Wear that brand of clothing. Or drive this kind of car..." We want to be "encouraged", even if it means deceiving ourselves. We can't live long without running into a lie in one form or another. We love them! Who can pass up a street magic show, or not be arrested by an optical illusion? In nature there are just as many deceptions - from rock encrusted dragonfly larva to fake eyes on moth wings or tiger ears.

Then, there's the knack we have for fooling ourselves. The 'Self-deception', found in some addictive thought processes, is another level of deceit. The addict convinces himself that, in spite of the negative consequences, there is sufficient 'reward' to repeat the behaviour. The reward, stimulates the release of hormones in the brain that alter the addicts reality and eases the 'pain' of their unaltered state. Humans are not alone in this realm. Every social species animal seeks an *altered reality* in one way or another.

Ruffed grouse and wasps imbibing on over ripe berries in the fall and Moose stumbling through urban streets, drunk on fermenting apples, top the list for animal 'substance' abuse. The *new* trend of obsessive behaviours, diagnosed in today's pet populations, is as far as we need to look for comrades-in-addiction.

Deception has played an integral part in the evolution of both plants and animals. It can make your head swirl if you meditate on the progression of that one quality, from primordial swamp to its current place in our modern world - necessity being the mother of invention and all. If we consider deception as a vital part of a species evolutionary success, it would seem likely that behaviours, etched in those organisms as a result, would be naturally inclined to its purposeful use in acquiring physical or emotional needs. In other words an irrevocable 'survival skill'.

Looking at our own species dependence on lies isn't a pleasant subject. But it gets easier if we can understand that, like so many of our emotions, the trait or tradition, if you want to call it that, is something much older than we are as a species. Arguments have been made that define animal produced lies as being, free of conscious thought and based in survival instincts that were evolved to maintain the animal's most essential needs. In that light, it would be logical to conclude that, like base emotions, and those fight-or-flight type instincts founded in the limbic system of the brain, Lies too may stem from primal forces, but then grow in complexity and effectiveness, through tweaks of the conscious mind.

* * *

Lets think about the lowly chicken for a second or two.

A low ranking rooster, in a large flock, can be seen to scratch the ground, flap his wings to draw attention to himself, and then cluck to a hen, telling her he's got some good stuff over here! A hen might leave the group, who are enamoured by the current cock-of-the-walk. The lonely rooster will peck the ground to show her where his stash is.

When she arrives, she'll peck in the area he was indicating. Likely there isn't, nor was there ever, anything 'good' there, but it's lured her away from the top bird and lonely rooster isn't lonely anymore. His lie worked.

In order for the rooster to be able to formulate his plan, he would have had to think out a few things:

1. Identify his emotional need - he was alone and needed to change that

2. Select a target - he wanted company but, in particular that of a hen, not another rooster

3. Understand another's "needs" - to use as bait - what it is that will make the hen come to him

4. Deceive her. He had nothing she might want, so he has to 'create' the illusion that he does have something - hence the scratching, clucking, and wing flapping

5. Assess risk, whether the top rooster is going to let him get away with it, or is he going to have to beat it to save his tail feathers!

Each step, to some degree, required that he

premeditate, plan, and execute falsehoods. A little more involved than a survival-based neurological reaction to a stress situation. It indicates abilities of forethought and somewhat of an *ego*, a simplified version of our own yet, present none the less.

The ability to recognize ourselves in a mirror is fertile ground for the growth of our most cerebral manifestation, the ego. With an ego the size of a human beings', it's difficult to not manifest deceptions. We're smart, can reason, can compare logical facts, can assess actions against consequences, and still be creative enough to effectively deceive ourselves.

Our species' gift of self-perception exacerbates our instinctual propensity for using lies. Like no mammal before, we have taken deception to an all new extreme. A lion trainer deceives the cat into believing the man is bigger, stronger, faster, kinder, and safer than the animal can be without him. In a similar more subtle way, man developed many belief systems to ratify and soothe questions or fears of the afterlife, morals and our place in the universe.

When we think of human beings lying, we think of a lie that we've been told or have told. "Santa Claus is coming to town," or when we ask a visibly dejected person, "How are you" and get the "I'm fine!" response. Often, the progression of a lie begins with a verbal statement, which is given away as not being true by nonverbal cues.

These nonverbal signs are detected by our senses. Our

brains are always busy analyzing incoming data, and notices anomalies. The body language or the facial expression does not support the dialogue, etc. Most of the time we don't become fully conscious of what that anomaly was, but we receive an unconscious emotional response that tells us '*something ain't right!*' Most times we let these emotions go as 'hunches', or 'feelings', that we've been misled. Without "proof" we're left with uncertainty. The field of forensic interviewing is one area where these hunches and feelings have been turned into scientific-based certainties. We do not fully understand the capabilities of our brain, nor its functions, but it's certain that, from one end of the body to the other, it's all connected. Physically or emotionally, if it's there, there's a reason for its presence.

An experiment was performed to see if there was a connection between leadership skills and lying abilities. Test subjects were given two tasks.

The first activity required individuals to sit in front of a camera, take a sip of a new soft drink, and make a video commercial touting the sweet taste of the product.

The beverage they were given to drink, while the camera rolled, was not sweet, but very sour. They had to follow their script and lie about what they had just tasted. The footage revealed a few exceptionally talented liars. But the vast majority of participants were unconvincing in their performance.

The second test was structured so that the subjects were

split into groups. The groups were tasked with building a structure out of drinking straws. A prize would be awarded to the group who could build the tallest structure.

Within the group dynamic, under time constraints and with a prize in jeopardy, it wasn't long before group hierarchy kicked in. Leaders emerged with profound results.

The best drink salesmen were the most likely to become the group leaders.

Animals can demonstrate some uncanny lying abilities as well...

Dozer

Dozer was the first 'great' dog I ever had. He was a show standard, yellow Labrador who walked with the charisma of a canine John Wayne. Even people who didn't like dogs loved him. He was the quintessential white knight of dogs. He was also the first dog that showed me how proficient they can be at lying.

His first 'lies' were created as part of a floor show we developed for guests, at a mountain resort where we lived. Aside from a bunch of cute parlour tricks, we had a routine where I'd talk with him and he'd answer with barks and *looks*.

* * *

"Dozer, do you have a girlfriend?" I'd ask him.

"Woof!" He'd answer back, his eyes bright, ears as <u>up</u> as a flop eared dog can get them.

"Do you want a snack?"

"Woof!"

Doze, were you in the garbage?"

He'd drop his nose, wrinkle his brow, and look away to an interesting place on the floor. Looking, for all the world, like a poor woe-begotten scapegoat.

There were a couple other 'negative' questions, that I could throw in, that would cause him to react in the "who me?" fashion. The crowd loved it. But it was a routine, not so much a real 'lie'.

The first obvious lie he told, occurred one time when we had finished filming for the day, and the crew was standing around talking in a small group. Dozer was bored waiting for me. I noticed him looking away from the group, toward a lake about a hundred yards from where we stood. He loved to swim. So, while he stared at the water, I told him to "go on, have a swim". He didn't have to be told twice, and headed off at a slow trot to the water.

Show standard Labs are notoriously lazy creatures. Dozer was no different. When he reached the top of the pitch going down to the shore, I saw him stop. The hill down to the lake was steep and lined with large, pit-run type boulders, not comfortable to walk on. I saw him glance back over his shoulder, to where we stood, then he changed his mine and headed off into the trees on an alternative adventure.

About five minutes later he emerged onto the trail from the bushes, right where he had left it. I saw him and called to him "Hey! What are you doing? I thought I told you to go swimming?"

He stood looking at me for a long second, and then shook his coat as if he was wet.

He'd lied.

At that time we were at a stage of training that very behaviour to a cue. He would do it reliably when he was wet after a swim but had not completed a real 'dry shake'. Instead, in the past, he had pretended to confuse my hand signals for "Shake" with the hand command I used for "speak", and would bark instead of shaking his whole body.

There he had stood "shaking" the non-existent water off his coat, that was on him from the swim he was supposed to have just taken. I laughed to myself and called him. He jogged over, not a concern showing in his countenance for having failed to comply with my command. When he got to me, I gave him the cue for "shake" again.

* * *

His eyes got big for a second, he opened his mouth to bark, and then you could see him "Remember" his lie, and for the first time ever "Shook" like he was wet.

It could have been chance that he felt like shaking after coming out of the forest. Maybe some dirt or pine needles were poking his back. But the timing of it was wrong. He waited to shake until after I had reminded him of swimming. It could also have been chance that, for the first time, on the shores of a lake, he "shook" when asked instead of barking. I didn't believe in chance playing a role then, nor do I now. More dogs have shown me their ability to lie since then. Most carry out more subtle lies, without too much thought involved on the dog's part, but they're lies just the same.

If we're good at reading our own species language, verbal and nonverbal, we'll be all the more prepared to read a different species dialect. If we can learn to see through more of our own species deceptions, we'll be better able to detect our animals', sometimes feigned, conditions. If we can detect and read emotional states, we can take the steps to soothe or encourage - depending on the animal's <u>True</u> needs (physical or emotional).

Like learning any other language, cross-species communication requires commitment, study, and practise. Our dogs are forgiving and appreciate our efforts, even if we do talk their language with a funny 'accent.'

Shared Needs

Eckman identified seven emotions that are 'global' and can be seen anywhere there are humans. These global emotions are depicted in facial expressions, regardless of geographic, genetic, or societal backgrounds. Again, the emotions he's defined are: happy, sad, anger, surprise, fear, disgust, and contempt. We can create the facial expression for any of these base emotions, by just thinking the name of one of them. We can just as easily conjure up body language that would naturally *accessorize* the facial expression.

If we look to each of the base emotions in Eckman's list, and consider how they developed in association with our emotional needs evolution, and how those need's developed acquisition skills, it's just a small step back down the trunk of the evolutionary tree to come to the conclusion that we operate from a set of emotions and a base *language*, that is older than we are as a species.

Our methods of communicating are rich. Language is the foundation of relationships, and fundamental in how we fit within larger social circles. Trust, faith, love, or any other emotion we feel toward another, is rooted in our deciphering of those signals we receive from others and how our perception of them is shaped.

We could go so far as to allude to our emotions and language skills, as connecting us to a grander global language. One that goes beyond dialect, geography, or species.

* * *

Language evolved, like our other skills, as a way to increase the chances of an organism's survival. Social species animals required more elaborate communication skills, than non-social species. From alarm signals, to resource sharing, to mating, herd animals developed signals to help them meet their inborn needs.

For our own species, those needs were best summarized by Joe Griffin and Ivan Tyrrell, in their 2004 book <u>Human Givens: A New Approach to Emotional Health and Clear Thinking</u>. They list a set of *given needs* that we're all born with. These innate needs develop as a result of instinctual patterns carried from one generation to the next, at a genetic level. Their list resembles the 'given' needs of many social species animals.

The Wikipedia summary for their list of 'Human Givens needs," is as follows:

"The basic assumptions of the Human Givens approach are that humans have evolved innate physical and emotional needs called 'human givens'. Human beings instinctively seek to meet these needs in their environment. When a person's innate needs are met in the environment, he or she will flourish. When these needs are not met in a balanced way, mental distress results... The emotional needs include:

*- **Security** – safe territory and an environment which allows full maturity and development*

*- **Attention** (to give and receive it) – a form of "mental nutrition"*

*- Sense of **autonomy and control** – having volition to*

make responsible choices
- *Being **emotionally connected** to others*
- *Feeling **part of a wider community***
- ***Friendship** and intimacy with someone who is accepting of the total person, flaws included*
- ***Privacy** – opportunity to reflect and consolidate experience*
- *Sense of **status** within social groupings*
- *Sense of **competence and achievement***
- ***Meaning and purpose"***

If we compare this list with the "Five freedoms" criterion, adopted by many humane organizations as guidelines for animal care, the similarities are obvious:
- ***Freedom from hunger or thirst*** by ready access to fresh water and a diet to maintain full health and vigour
- ***Freedom from discomfort*** by providing an appropriate environment, including shelter and a comfortable resting area
- ***Freedom from pain, injury, or disease*** by prevention, or rapid diagnosis and treatment
- ***Freedom to express normal behaviour*** by providing sufficient space, proper facilities, and company of the animal's own kind
- ***Freedom from fear and distress*** by ensuring conditions and treatment which avoid mental suffering

The latter was developed in 1965, and is sometimes referred to as Brambell's Five Freedoms: it's a common-sense, minimalistic set of codes of practise for animal husbandry. Hints of the Human Givens' needs can be seen, in this simplified version, as an accepted animal care mandate.

Understanding our own needs helps us to empathize with our animals. It gives us a deeper understanding and enables us to more appropriately respond, communicate, and provide for them.

Ancient Similarities

The forerunners of domestic animals were originally targeted by our ancestors, because the herds lived and interacted in ways similar to our own. This enabled early man to predict the animal's needs, motivations, and actions. This improved chances for successful hunts, safe passage through predator's territories, or surviving whatever multi-species interactions their environment threw their way. During the domestication process social animal's needs were visible and understandable to early man. They could then ensure the animal's dependence by manipulating the environment and providing for those innate needs. Eventually, selective breeding muted the animal's own natural drives and produced domesticated versions of what were once wild animals.

We are still capable of using those same skills our primitive forefathers did. To this day we can be shown, for the first time, a social species animal in its natural environment. Most people could make good guesses about the animal's condition and disposition. We can garner visual information that gives us clues to: age of the animal (juvenile, adult, senior), physical health (condition of the coat, body mass, gait and demeanour) and, if other members of its group are in proximity, we might even be able to figure out which animal was the leader.

This ancient gift, stems from being able to associate similarities between ourselves and other species. An infant animal is smaller than an adult one, an older animal may be hunched or lamed with arthritis, etc... These comparisons are sometimes minimized as being anthropomorphic, though it's more plausible that, like our base emotions, this latent skill is older than we are as a species. If wolves can draw from their instincts to deduce which caribou they should target, is it so strange to consider that we too retain some of this natural ability?

Living in an urban world accounts for the vast majority of our population's habitat. People, amid the hustle and bustle of an urban setting, cannot maintain a connection to nature. Every city has its trees and parks, but the nature I'm speaking of is one in which the experience is free from the hubbub. No hum of high voltage power lines, no road noise, a sky devoid of planes. Just the sounds of nature... The Wilds.

For the majority of today's people, a place in the 'wilds' would be a traumatic experience. Our new urban roots, of the past 100 years, have removed generations of people from the experience that such a place can provide. The rights-of-passage ceremonies of earlier cultures have gone by the wayside. Few youths participate in walkabouts, first hunts, or journeys marking their passage from childhood to adulthood. Urbanized man has no counterpart that allows for the development of personal inner realizations of one's strengths and abilities. The results we see in today's societies mark our own self-domestication. Children live at home into their mid-twenties and beyond, to the degree that legislation in some places has been rewritten to increase the age of dependency to 25 years of age. Similar to our ever-dependant domestic animals, we have disconnected from our own "wild-side" and entered into a muted life, devoid of that connection we once relied upon for our survival. It's justified as progress and civil, yet grows discontent and puts us ill-at-ease with ourselves. Those old instinctual patterns that our species evolved with, are still in us, but for lack of stimulation in a way that hones the skills they were meant to promote, we find ourselves living in a society fraught with anxiety, depression, and addiction. Many suffer undefined 'dis-eased' existences, without the foggiest idea why.

In today's humming world of electricity and combustion engines, it's hard to not 'disconnect' from all but our most essential instincts and abilities. The input generated from urban stimuli, means something has to go! Even with our huge brains, simple economics comes into play. If a skill or inherited gift is not used, the ability may wither away or mutate and become malignant. In many cases the lack of nature in the human's life more directly affects their dog. When the person is unable to relate to the rhythms and realities of an unplugged world their ability to adequately provide the attention and focus needed to support their pet is compromised.

* * *

Wild and domestic animals can remind us so much about language and our self. They can remind us of where we come from, and show us new ways to see things. They can show us of how simplicity can be calming, wholesome and fulfilling. They can share with us in their own language and behaviour a certain wisdom many of us have lost or forgotten.

One of the oddest forms of cross-species dialogue I've witnessed, occurred between a horse and a bear on the shores of Kakwa Lake, in the Rocky Mountains near the British Columbia/Alberta border. We had camped at the lake for some days. Our transportation consisted of 15 pack and saddle horses. One morning, after lighting the fire and having breakfast, we sat planning our day, with the cabin door open. Sunlight streamed in and cast a warm ambiance that matched the view of the mountains, mist in the meadow, and our grazing horses. Our lead mare was tethered on a long line, about 150 feet from our cabin door. She was a sage old horse, having first been brought to the area when she was a suckling foal. It was a rare pastoral scene.

We, humans spotted the bear first. In spite of all our talking, wood smoke, and gear, a big grizzly bear had taken his morning drink from the clear lake then, without concern for anything in his way, set off toward his next destination. His route took him between our tethered mare and the front door of our cabin.

A second or two after we noticed the lumbering bear, he turned his head toward the horse. The mare had been eating grass, facing the cabin; she had to have seen the bear, but had continued to eat. The moment the bear stopped walking, the horse lifted her head, slowly bringing it up to a natural position. Nothing in how she moved, indicated that she was frightened, nor was there any facial indication that she was stressed by the big bear's presence. Across the distance the two looked at each other. Bears don't see well, and it was unlikely that he could make out too clearly what the white movement had been, but scent or noise told him what was there - or he just didn't care one way or the other. After a long pause, as if orchestrated, the bear turned to look back down the trail, and the mare lowered her head for another mouthful of grass. Neither of them with a hair out of place, or a smidgen of concern for the odd experience we'd all shared.

Whatever it was that the Bear said to the horse or vice versa - they understood each other's position and both went along their merry ways. No harm, no foul.

The ironic part of the bear and horse dialogue is that it went on between two very different species. Horses, like humans, are social by nature. Their dialogue is rich and their hierarchies well formed.

Bears are a non-social animal. Non-social species do not normally have the need for elaborate communications, nor do they draw beneficial experiences from contact with others of their own kind, aside from yearly matings or as infants under the care of their mothers.

Bears are an odd lot when it comes to non-social species animals. It seems their ability to communicate is enhanced by the length and time they are dependent on their mothers. They have been known to maintain contact with their mothers for upwards of 3 years before heading off on their mostly solitary lives.

In the opposite extreme, porcupine infants are perfunctorily given a shot of colostrum and sent on their way within a couple months of birth. Their language skills and intelligence are some of the most pitiful on the planet. Yet, they are still capable of simple communication between themselves and other species. Their lives are so boring (to us) that, until recently, very little was known about them. They'd spend a day or two up the same tree and, aside from noting their movements from one tree to the next, researchers could find very little of interest or of import about them − let alone anything interesting they might have to write about.

In the late 80's we had a job that called for wolves and a porcupine. I was a rookie trainer on the job, and tasked with maintaining the animals during transport. We had an infant porcupine with us, and he became a pet project while we drove across Canada.

Quinn, the porcupine, had been born in captivity, after his mother had been brought to the compound injured. As chance would have it, he had been born the next day and spent extra time 'unnaturally' close to his mother, nursing frequently and forming an unnaturally strong bond with her, that free living porcupines never develop.

For the first couple days of the trip he wouldn't eat, and was visibly upset, pacing in his cage and vocalizing. By the third day, I was concerned enough to risk taking him out of his cage to see if I could get him more comfortable. As it turned out, the little guy was just lonesome. He wanted to be touched, and feel the heat of another body. He crawled up on my lap and snuffled around, then settled into a spot, and closed his tired little eyes. Now that might sound all well and cute, but we are talking about a porcupine here. It didn't take me long to learn that little Quin-full-of-quills could only do one thing at a time.

If he was focused on social contact, he was very handle-able. We could slide our hands between his front legs, under his belly, and pick him up without him showing any alarm. But! If you asked him to do two things at once, it was highly unwise to move! I found his favourite road food to be lettuce and other bitter tasting vegetables. I'd pull him out of his cage and make him follow a bit of lettuce around. Once he had food in his grasp and was focused on eating it - that was it. If I moved a muscle, caused a shadow or a noise, his defence system went into full alert and his quills puffed up ready for action. Any further movement would cause the little bugger to flip around and strike with his tail, leaving behind a trail of sharp quills. His defence reactions would abate as quickly as they came. Once quiet returned, he'd toddle off in whatever direction called to him next.

* * *

He learnt a few behaviours on cue. Contrary to what was believed possible for the species at that time. He showed recognition of individuals, his name, and simple directional commands. His memory was pretty good, too. He would become excited every time he saw me, after that first road trip, even months after the fact. But in the grand scheme of things, his neural capabilities were very limited. A critter doesn't need huge intellect when it has the best defence system in the animal kingdom.

The range of intelligence and communication skills, in the natural world, varies to broad extremes. Each species has its own set of needs and appropriate skills with which to acquire the resources necessary to provide for those needs. If we honour those limits, skills, and needs, we can find natural ways to communicate with species that are not our own, enriching both species lives in the process.

Differences - Ears n' Tail or (Human limitations)

When we look at ourselves, side by side with other species, we are blessed in many ways, and limited in others. Our ability to speak makes up for many of those limitations, but when we look at our canine companions, they have two adaptations for communication that we cannot replicate or imitate. It's not surprising then, that these two attributes cause confusion in their meanings, for some of us humans.

Ear control

An animal's ear control, the ability to independently move one or both ears in a given direction, adds visual cues of intent or emotional state, that can be viewed from a distance. Dogs use these cues, in conjunction with other body postures, to announce feelings across a broad range of base emotions. Dogs possess the cognitive ability to 'decide' what to do with their ears. They can use them to present a truth, or to mask a deception. Their ears are also prone to giving away a deception, by unconsciously going against what the other parts of the body are saying – in essence, a component of a canine version of a 'micro-expression'.

For instance, a dog barking behind a fence might have a deep sounding bark, his posture may be imposing and threatening, his ears pricked forward, locked on a passing invader. If the invader abruptly challenges back, with noise, posture, or look, the dog might be intimidated, but hold the bluff of posture and bark together. But, if the dog momentarily drops his ears flat against his skull, you can be certain that at that moment, a doubt crept into his mind.

Tail Posture and Position

I've often wondered how or why some primates lost their tails. They seem like pretty good ideas, for the most part. Mind you, getting them caught in a car door would suck, so maybe it's not such a bad thing we're without.

In the case of our four legged friends, the tail certainly does tell the tale (I had to!). The dog's tail is one of the most animated and easily seen language components they possess.

An easy way to understand what a dog's tail position indicates is to imagine it as a dual purpose Security/ Confidence gauge. When it's down low to the ground or between their legs, it indicates low levels of security and/ or increased fear, low confidence. The more under the body and between the legs it is, the more *terror* is being experienced. As the tail is raised up from between their legs and goes into that stiff, still, posture that arches over their back, we reach the other extreme on the gauge that announces high levels of confidence and assertiveness potential. Either extreme of the gauge's travel should have little red sections that mark a warning, and must be met with caution. A dog with its tail consistently nearer the halfway mark, or horizontal with its spine, is a dog that is comfortable and relaxed – right where we want them.

Kai, a border collie we once had, was the most effective canine manipulator/communicator I've ever seen. I'd use her behaviour in classes, to demonstrate her passive means of dominating. With a group of 10 or more people, all seated and relaxed, I would turn Kai loose on them. She would come in low, usually working from left to right. Her body posture screamed "*I'm so happy to be here, but oh! I'm so nervous. Look, I'm not very confident either!*" Her ears would be pinned to her head, her tail low, hind quarters scrunched under her hip, head low and cast at a 45 degree angle from those she was nearest to. Her eyes would be soft and unchallenging.

Within a few short seconds, she would make the rounds of the group. She'd stop at each person, for just a fraction of a second, before moving on. She assessed each person she met. By the time she had completed her clockwise circuit, she would have made her decision. Next, she'd head directly to the person she had deduced was going to be the easiest to 'control'.

She'd approach her 'mark' with the same submissive posturing, elevating her deception with the use of lip licking, and nervous tail wags that brushed the ground behind her. She'd sit lightly in front of them, showing one side of her face then the other. She would shift her weight onto her front feet to create a rocking appearance. The difference in her language, now, was from her eyes. She would gaze into their eyes for longer periods, look away, and then look back. You could see her expecting the answer she wanted, which was an invite from that person to have contact. For Kai, that was when she knew she'd won. The instant the person reached out to pet her, the dog's passive manipulation tactics went into high gear. She'd work her way under their hand, beside their leg, then up onto the couch beside them, so sweet that butter wouldn't melt in her mouth. All the while she was doing this, her body would move constantly, wriggling and twitching her way as close to the person as she could get.

When she'd reached the position she wanted, leaning

against the human with her head slightly higher than the person's, she was done.

The eye contact that had flickered over the person's face stopped. Her wriggling stopped. All that remained was a self-satisfied look on a Border collie face, whose body reclined its full weight on her newest *follower*. Gone was the uncertain body language, her ears perked up and followed her steady, confident gaze, her tail arched out from underneath her hips, the little white tip of it flagged above her haunches. Her eyes no longer looked fearful or soft, instead they looked at the other participants so much as to say "There - Who's next?"

Hackles and eyes

For all our control over nonverbal communication components, we and our dogs have at least two of these that are beyond our mental and physical control.

Piloerection and dilation of the pupils

In humans, piloerection is better known as goosebumps, in dogs it's when their hackles go up.

Considering the shared history of our needs, motivations, and behaviours, it's safe to conclude that, raised hackles in dogs are caused by the same types of emotions that cause our goose-bumps. For us, goose-bumps indicate we're feeling a chill. But emotions can trigger their raising as well. Fear is the most common, but other heightened states of emotion can cause similar effects: sexual arousal, sadness, joy, or surprise.

Raised hackles mean that, the dog's current take on its environment is scaring it so bad its survival instincts have taken control and are attempting to make the dog appear bigger than it is. An instinctual mechanism evolved to try and avoid physical confrontation.

Fear and aggression are close neighbours, so it's easy to see how the two are often mixed up by humans. As in most cases of human aggression, canine aggression is usually the end result of an individual being too afraid. It's a fine line between fear and aggression, often dogs are seen to be 'aggressive' when in fact they started out as being scared and were pushed beyond their capacity to cope. Hackles are the warning we should be looking for, that tells us our pet is becoming stressed. Their limbic system is about to or already has taken control and they've lost the use of their 'big brains' and gone stupid (with fear).

The same is true of an animal's pupil dilation. Contrary to normal function, constricting and dilating to adjust to light levels, an animal's eyes are susceptible to psychological processes that demand the eye let in as much light as possible. This makes sure that nothing in the environment is missed, in times of danger, as well as in other times of heightened emotions.

With either raised hackles or 'black-eyed' dogs we must remember, that during such times of extreme emotion, our animals are not in their 'right mind'. During such a state, their behaviour can't be expected to be normal or 'rational'. Just as children having a temper tantrum cannot be 'forced' out of their state through intimidation, or by a parent demanding calm, neither can our dogs spontaneously end their heightened state of emotion. Instead, small steps are required to be taken, to avert their attention from the source of the elevated emotions.

We all have Accents

At this point in the session, most people are starting to feel their heads fill up from all my rambling. I assure them that it'll sink in, over the course of the next few days or weeks. Shifts in perspective take time to settle in and take root. For some people the shift happens right away, and within days they are enjoying a whole new level of enjoyment from their relationships.

Others take longer.

Sandra & Chance

One morning long ago, the shelter I worked at received a frantic call about an aggressive dog that was on a rural property. The caller said there were two dogs, but the second one was a little thing and didn't appear to be dangerous. They were anxious because they needed to get to work, but the big black dog wouldn't let them out of their house.

I was happy to be dispatched. It got me out of finishing the kennel chores.

During the half hour drive to the address, I had time to ruminate on what could cause a stray dog to claim a strange property and confine the inhabitants to their home. In a half hour all kinds of scenarios can play out in a person's head, and by the time I got to the location, I was no closer to guessing what was going on than when I'd started driving.

The driveway angled off the main road through dense forest. It was cloudy, and the grey light that filtered through put a gloomy tint to the neat little homestead carved out of the coastal rainforest. Two vehicles sat in the parking area, and I could see three faces watching from the kitchen window, that overlooked the steps leading up to the house. All was quiet when I put the truck in park and turned off the engine. I felt a twinge of disappointment with the silence. The stillness led me to think that the dogs had moved on. Before leaving the truck, I second guessed myself and reached for the catch-pole. I was new to the job, but not to working with dangerous animals.

Experience is a hard teacher, but once you learn her golden rule, you never forget it. That rule is: Expect the best, but always be prepared for the worst.

Ten steps away from the truck I was glad I'd brought the catch-pole with me. From where I'd parked, I hadn't been able to see the front door of the house. When I came around the vehicle that blocked the entrance from my sight, I caught a quick glimpse of two normal looking, relaxed dogs. The little one looked like a Shitzu cross. She had a scruffy black and grey, matted coat and was sitting there staring at the door, as if waiting to be let inside. Beside her, lying down on the porch, with his nose pointed in her direction, was the black lab. It was a quick look at these relaxed dogs, because in the next second, they both heard my feet scuff in the gravel.

Both dogs charged me at once. It was surreal, scary and funny all at once.

The little dog bounced toward me like I was her long lost pal. The Big lab came barking at me on stiff legs, with hackles raised. He was good at being intimidating. I saw right away why these usually self-sufficient country folk had called!

The black dog kept himself a few feet behind the little one, and followed her to where I stood. The shitzu jumped up on my shins, snorting through crooked little teeth. She was thrilled that I was there. I couldn't really afford the time or attention to give her a return greeting. The big guy still growled and barked a continual string of rhythmic "woo-woo-woo" threats. I lowered the end of the catch-pole to a little below his eye level and kept it between us, while the little dust-mop begged to be picked up.

The rhythm and tone of the black Lab's bark, and the way he held his place behind the little dog, tallied up in my limbic system to a "Not so bad" rating on my Chances for Survival Checklist. I was able to think and start figuring out how I was going to solve the problem.

* * *

Not during the half hour drive out there, nor likely over the course of a lifetime, could I have guessed what had caused the people to be trapped in their house by a fifteen pound lap dog and a black lab cross. The little shitzu-cross was in heat! Her Black Knight wasn't about to let anything get between him and his true love. All she wanted was a warm place to sleep and something to eat.

The rhythm of his bark gave him away. He wasn't that much of a bad guy. A dog that barks the way he was, might take a chomp out of you, but the type of bite will differ from a dog that just walks up slowly, head held low, and grumbles barely audible bass-filled growls: those ones, you really don't want to get involved with! The woo-woo-woo that my adversary threw at me wasn't convincing at all. If I turned my back on him, he'd probably have given my arse a little nip, but I felt confident that, as long as I didn't take my eyes off him, he wouldn't have the courage to test the stick with the dangling cord, I held between us.

I side-stepped my way back to where my truck was parked. The little dog trailed at my feet, and the barking Lab followed a few feet beyond the end of the catch-pole. I lifted the canopy door and opened the tailgate. The little shitzu was in a good position, so I didn't wait or think about it too much. I reached down, scooped her up with my free arm, and set her on the tailgate of the truck.

The Lab didn't like that, not even a little bit. He upped the volume of his bark and moved around the catch-pole to get nearer the little dog. That was about the time I heard a voice, from the far side of the vehicle, next to where I'd parked.

"You need a hand?" a male voice inquired.

In a situation like this, it's always bad enough to worry about your own neck, but to add the three people from the kitchen window to the mix was a little much. Thankfully, the Lab had more immediate concerns. He didn't leave me to chase them back into the house. I politely declined the offer.

I gave the little shitzu's head a tussle, and backed away from her and the truck. This gave the Lab a chance to go up and give her a sniff, to make sure she was still the same girl he loved.

A catch-pole is a long, adjustable length pole, with a coated cable running up the inside of it, that comes out of the business end in a loop that can be dropped over a fractious animal's head, and tightened up with a quick pull. The Lab was so smitten with his little beauty, that he didn't notice my first attempt to get the loop over his head. The second time I missed, he moved away from the truck and took to barking at me again. I didn't want him transferring onto the spectators, so I backed off again and let him go back to his sweetheart. For the third try, I made the loop as big as it could be, and got lucky when I flipped it over his nose. He put up a fine bit of a fight for a couple seconds, but his focus cleared when I used the pole to push him 'Away' from little Miss Shitzu. The pole and noose around his neck weren't hurting, but being bodily removed from his heart's desire did. When I moved out of his line of sight, away from the truck where, with much thanks, the little shitzu stood watching from the tailgate, he made a bee-line back to her. As he went, I slid my left hand up the catch-pole, half-way to where the Lab's head was, and lowered the handle so I could put my free, right arm over the top of it. When he had almost reached the truck, I started lifting on his neck with the catch-pole. I clamped the free end of it under my right armpit as I encircled his belly, and used his momentum to pick him up off the ground and into the box of the truck; a single, flowing movement. It happened so fast the Lab hardly noticed being lifted. Holding him away from me with the pole, I closed up the tailgate and locked the canopy door. Crisis over!

The Lab, Chance, he would eventually be called, had been a hormonal basket case when I first met him. Popcorn, his little girlfriend, and he had been on the run for days; chased away from each house she led them to, after Chance tried to demonstrate his claim to her. They'd both been raised in the boonies, and Chance had never been anything more than a kick-about lawn ornament. When Popcorn's pheromones got his own mating hormones raging, Chance wasn't a very friendly fella.

When we got them settled down in separate kennel runs, Chance calmed down and regained some of his senses. I had only one minor 'argument' with him over who owned the bowl of food in his kennel, and from that time on he was my dog. His owners never came to claim him, and he wound up a resident at the shelter for almost a year. He was neutered and fell into the kennel routine quite well. He became one of my best helpers for socializing skittish or aggressive new dogs. The nasty 'stray dog' he'd been when he arrived, was forgotten.

Then one day I came into work, after being away on holidays, and Chance was gone. He'd found a home. A happy ending, or so it seemed!

A month or two later I received a call, at home, from a distraught dog owner from Victoria, who had adopted a dog and had run into some problems. She told me that she'd been to a Trainer and a Vet, specializing in behaviour, and both had warned her to euthanize the dog, for fear that he would not only injure others, but her as well. Somehow she'd found my number for training and called in a last ditch attempt to resolve her problems. It took us a little while to figure out that the dog she had adopted was Chance. We booked the appointment for the next day.

She showed up early.

The old red Volvo pulled in with a lot of barking from the back seat. Sandra got out wearing her signature African fez hat. She was about forty years old, tall, slim, and anxious. She'd been anxious a while, so much so, that after one traumatic incident in her life, she'd lost every hair on her body. Chance was in the back seat, reminding me of what he'd been like the first day I met him.

They were a mess, but they'd grown to love each other,

in the short time they'd been together, and Sandra wasn't about to listen to the experts that had told her they feared for her safety.

Before she brought Chance out of the car, I listened to her version of what had happened to bring them to where they were. She said that Chance had growled and snapped at a few people, but had not actually bitten anyone.

My kids were running around the farm, playing with the chickens and sheep that were in the pasture. Sandra was shocked when I told her to let him out, so we could go for a walk in the fields.

"I'll leash him up though, right?" she asked.

"No." I said. "This is Chance, right? He'll be okay. You'll have to trust me."

She gave me a doubting look so I continued, "In the shelter, he was my dog, he'll be alright, let him out."

The contradiction between the last two people she'd sought help from caused her a lot of indecision, but she eventually gave me her trust and turned my old pal out of the car. He came over to me and we had a short greeting, then I started leading the way into the pasture where the sheep and horses milled with the chickens in the warm morning sunlight.

"Are you sure we shouldn't put a leash on him? Has he

ever been around sheep before?" Sandra asked, while she tried to keep up to the dog and me.

"I don't know. Come on, he's fine", I called to her over my shoulder.

Sandra's disbelief grew as we walked among the sheep. Her 'killer dog' was relaxed, and focused solely on being beside me. He ignored all the livestock, and was in every way, a perfect gentleman.

Sandra had a brilliant mind, degrees in art, and computer sciences, among other things. Over the course of the next hour and a half, we went through the why's and how's of keeping Chance calm and safe.

It didn't work!

She came back for a full weekend clinic of intense training and theory. That didn't work either.

Next she made the drive up, on a weekly basis, for a popular series of 'Drop-in' sessions we offered.

Sandra and Chance were a challenge. I knew both sides of the dog, and how easy he was to control. Sandra was diligent and had learnt everything I'd taught her, by rote. She could repeat it back, and talk concepts of training fluently. I couldn't be sure why she was having such a difficult time with him.

Things got worse.

Chance nipped a person, then bit another while in her care. Sandra was losing hope and faith. All I could do was guess at what was holding them back, and keep up my mantra of how she had to convince Chance she was the Mother and that her word was the law. Failing that she needed do the responsible thing and have him put down.

Before she lost all her hair, she had been a red-head. I told her she needed to tap into that fiery side of herself, and be 'honest' with the dog. I told her I suspected she was somehow holding herself back from expressing herself in such a way that Chance could understand and believe, beyond contestation, that she meant what she said to him.

When the next Drop-in session started and Sandra didn't show up, I started to worry. She'd been a regular all summer, and wasn't one to be late. The drop-ins were designed to give city dogs the opportunity to come out to the country and experience fun, nature oriented, play, with a small bit of training interspersed for good measure. It was popular and there were sometimes, up to 15 dogs and their people cruising around the farm. Most were encouraged to have their dog off-leash, provided they were safe with the other animals and people. Sandra had always kept Chance on a leash, during these events.

When she arrived, fifteen or twenty minutes late, the whole crew of regulars could see there was something different. I think the dogs even stopped running around. She parked in a different place than usual and rummaged around inside her vehicle for a while, before getting out.

When she did exit the car, she sprang out, closed her door and smiled at us all. Next, she turned and opened the back door for Chance. He dropped to the ground and stood looking up at her, while she closed the door. Together they walked toward us, Sandra beamed, and Chance walked beside her, off leash, on a perfect 'heel', his eyes didn't leave her face.

I called to her from a good distance, "Hey Sandra! How's it going?"

Her step was lively and she smiled wider when she called back to me, "It's a new world order!"

After months of learning and digesting, she'd made the shift in perspective. Chance had bitten again, and Sandra had been there when it happened. She embraced the Momma wolf in her, and became who Chance needed her to be. The moment wasn't a pleasant one for anyone involved, least of all her friend, who Chance had chomped. But the incident was the impetus she needed to go-for-broke. Chance ceased to be a danger to anyone, from that point on. Sandra became his be-all-end-all stress reliever, to the point where he didn't even feel compelled to bark when someone knocked on her door. Sandra became an ardent problem dog rescuer, and helped other people and dogs surmount problems. It just took her a long time to make the shift, and become proficient at nonverbal communication.

It was actually because of a discussion we'd had about an experiment she had tried with Chance later on, that inspired my actions with Porter, the dog from the first story.

Her experiment had started when we talked about the difference in conflict resolution skills between humans and dogs. I'd told her that, when a dog watched two people have an argument, it sees, hears, and feels, the tension, and knows there is a conflict. When most couple's or people argue, it's a verbal confrontation, and from the dog's point of view, when the argument is over, the dog can't figure out who exactly won.

That discussion got Sandra thinking and she enrolled the help of one of her big burly biker friends. She prearranged the event, and made sure everything was set up perfectly. Chance was in the room, the big guy got there and then Sandra started a mock 'argument'. She waited until the fellow was standing in front of a chair and the tension had built. She said Chance had watched from his bed, and hadn't moved. When she felt the tension and atmosphere in the room was high enough, she made a show of physically forcing the big guy onto the low chair, and finished the scenario in a visibly dominant position over top the much bigger man.

Sandra laughed for years about the effect that one charade had on Chance. She said afterwards, he had looked and behaved toward her with much more respect, and increased his submissive signals to her as he never had before. The results of her work lasted as long as their relationship did.

* * *

The ethereal language that is native to social species animals is forgiving and understanding. It's like one language, spoken with vastly different accents. If we listen long and hard enough, we can pick up the rhythm and tempo, and then the words will start to pop out. We begin to understand.

With more practise, we can start to imitate the accent. For us and our domestic animals, this is when we start to communicate in a natural way.

CHAPTER FOUR

The Truth About Control

The Steering Wheel

At this point in the session, my audience is usually becoming glassy-eyed. I empathize with them. I've made them do a lot of thinking in a short time. To give them a little break from all the philosophy we've been talking about, we quickly discuss how all this knowledge can be put into play, and used as an effective 'steering wheel' for their dogs.

Just as with driving, we are tasked with doing several things at once, to keep things on an even course. Instead of accelerator, brake, and steering wheel, we can 'direct' our animal's motion and behaviour with a combination of language, timing, and pressure: colouring it all with our verbal and non-verbal <u>tones</u>.

The best way to show clients the effects of pressure and the use of good timing, is to demonstrate how even the most ardent leash-pulling dog will walk with a slack leash, under moderate distraction settings, within a few minutes. Using just a flat collar and a leash, without harsh corrections, treats, or coercion. In short, the dog is allowed to decide how it wants to walk, with or without pressure. Once it understands that it has a choice, it walks along content to avoid unnecessary pressure.

This chapter will focus on those skills mentioned above, and discuss the principals behind teaching our animals to live and learn in a human world.

Timing

The talent of what, in humans, is often described as "Having good timing", is crucial in almost all areas of our lives. Who hasn't seen someone with "no timing" flopping around on a dance floor, like a fish out of water? Knowing when to: flip the egg, jay-walk on a busy street, or when to close your fingers to catch a ball. Timing is visible and tangible, though sorely under appreciated. To the trained eye, timing is visible in our gait when walking or running, in our voice when speaking, and in our body language. My mentor and good friend, Gerry Therrien, renowned Hollywood film trainer, director, wild exotic and indigenous animal behaviour expert, has held to his mantra of: "Timing is the essence of life", for as long as I've known him. The deeper you ruminate on that statement, the more validity it gains.

Gerry was also responsible for introducing me to an exercise I have taught to clients for decades. The <u>Trainer's</u>

<u>Game</u> demonstrates the importance of timing, and how it relates to communication. The exercise involves a pen and paper, and something with which to make a simple sound: a dog clicker, two rocks to bang together, a pair of spoons, anything that can be relied upon to make a short simple sound. The game is a version of the old "Hot - Cold" children's game. It is played the same way, with "Hot" replaced with the simple sound or "click".

The Clicker operator or trainer, will write down the task they have in mind say, "bring the coffee pot to the table and fill my cup." The rules are simple:

1. No eye or body gestures are allowed by the trainer
2. The trainer must be silent
3. The trainer's only form of communicating is the clicker
4. When the task is completed the round is over - reverse roles for full effect
(Playing Tip: click - "hotter" - with each movement the subject makes in the right direction)

Start playing simple games like 'fetch' to develop player's skills. More difficult tasks require no objects, but demand the subject to contort their bodies into positions: sit down, cross your legs one way, cross your arms the other way, and stick your tongue out. As explained above, the premise is simple, yet surprisingly difficult to carry out. With practise, over a few days, the learning curve increases and timing improves significantly. It's hard to motivate adults to persevere for a week or two of playing 'kids' games, but the benefit to self-awareness is worth the effort.

This game can create the same emotional responses we experience, while trying to train our animals a new behaviour. If the trainer in the game misses a click, or clicks too late after the subject has altered their course, it can be a long, frustrating while before they are back on course. This game increases empathy, by providing the subject, being guided through the task, with an uncanny perspective of how our animals are affected by our, often untimely and incomprehensible, modes of communicating our demands to them.

Timing was the key to training the rats for the film, "The Bone Collector" in 1999. The director, Phillip Noyce, wanted BIG rats, but had to settle for a hundred old, retired, breeding rats from a laboratory in one of the Northern states. I'd been called in at the last minute, and wasn't overly enthused by the prospects of spending the next couple months with a bunch of old, un-handled rats. The rats were shipped to Vancouver, and I grudgingly met them there. I'd never worked with rats and, quite frankly, they gave me the creeps just looking at them crawling around their large travelling container.

The first task at hand was moving them from their transport container and separating them into isolated housing units. My aversion to the rats stemmed from societal impressions I'd unconsciously collected over the years. Risking ridicule and endless ribbing, I used gloves to handle the 'unclean' little critters. In that first contact, with one of the world's most hated rodents, my opinion of them started to change.

I lifted the first few out of the roiling mass of bodies by the tail. It didn't feel right handling them like that, so I started scooping them out of the container with my gloved hand, like we'd pick up a small pup or kitten with one hand. This different way of handling them had marked difference in how they behaved, when removed from the container. They calmed, and didn't squirm or squeak. What amazed me the most was that not one of the rats I picked up tried to bite the glove that held them: these old rats, housed in large, over-crowded pens, for their whole life, seldom if ever handled by humans, accepted my man-handling without retaliation or complaint.

My appreciation for their social and mental abilities continued to grow during the entire project. Of the one hundred rats, four emerged from the group and became "Star" rats. In two weeks I could appreciate each animal's unique personality, and had witnessed how quickly they achieve a state of conditioned response to stimuli, compared to any other species I'd ever worked. Where six weeks is the norm for achieving this degree of learning, rats seem to reach this state in around 10 days. No wonder they are so adaptable.

By the time we landed in Montreal for the shoot, I had nothing but appreciation for my furry little charges. The heebie-jeebies were long gone.

In this instance, teaching the rats was more of an education for the teacher than for the students. I had long appreciated the different personalities that individual animals possess, but this project instilled an appreciation for the plasticity and intelligence of an animal I had feared and loathed.

The script for the "Bone Collector" called for a number of rats to scurry along a beam, then jump down onto a 'Victim', who was tied to a piece of machinery. To prepare for the scene, the rats were clicker trained, Simple translation: they were taught that a sound meant "Food!"and if they hurried to it they'd find a reward.

To start with, I set up a table with six inch walls around the edge, like a wee rat fence. I then put a rat on the table, letting it cruise around for a while before chasing it down with a spoonful of canned pet food. None of them wanted to be caught again, after being released from their cages (can't blame them for that!). When they realized I was 'after them', they'd head for a corner of the table where there was a shadow. Once they'd backed into their best available hiding place, I'd approach them with the spoon. At first, fear dampened their appetites and they were only mildly interested in the food I'd stick in front of their noses. To make matters worse for them, I was waiting to see their mouths open to take a lick or a bite out of the meat, the instant they did, I would 'Click' and they'd jump back from the spoon and the noise.

Timing was everything, at this point. If I clicked a fraction of a second too soon, before the rat tasted the food, the foreign sound would scare it more, causing it to associate the scary 'new' sound with its own approach to the food, or worse, the food itself. In the opposite way, if I waited until the rat had too big a mouthful before I clicked, it would bolt to a different corner of the table and eat its food, without appreciating the connection between the sound of the clicker and the food-spoon.

When you have a hundred rats to work with, you get in a lot of practise in a very short time. Within a couple days, the four Star rats were beginning to stick out of the crowd. They progressed from learning that the sound of the clicker meant "Here's the Grub!", to finding the food by following the sound of the clicker.

We then changed 'sounds', switching from the rectangular plastic clickers popular in animal training for everything from dolphins to dogs, to an electronic beeper that we could operate remotely. Within a short time, the table with the little rat fence-surround, could be loaded up with blocks of wood to create a maze, and the rats would run through it, following the sound of the beeper, as it guided them through ever changing intersections and corners. They learned the game faster and better than I was able to play it with them! Once they were given a 'beep', that told them they were headed in the right direction, they would run as fast as they could to the next cross-roads, then stop and look one direction, then another. When their nose was pointed in the right direction, I'd 'beep' that they were looking the right way, and off they'd go to the next junction. Within ten days the four Star rats could be guided through a maze or 'room', as if they were remote-controlled.

* * *

The rat's ability to learn at an advanced age, was impressive, and did wonders to dispel much of my unconscious aversion to them. It wasn't until we were finally on set and working, that I fully appreciated the degree of their social nature, and how adept rats are at forming relationships. As well, how good they are at identifying individuals of a different species.

The scenes we were shooting were in an abandoned warehouse along the St. Lawrence River. The outside temperature was around freezing, so it was quite the chore to keep our animal actors warm. We set up a warm, enclosed, 'rat' trailer to house and transport them to and from locations. Our crew of Montreal based rat-wranglers consisted of three men and a woman. The girl took it upon herself to be the rats' momma; feeding, cleaning, and nurturing the group in between shots.

At one point, we were discussing the next shot, lights were being set up and the crew was adjusting gear. I'd brought in "Blondie," one of the Star rats, so that the camera could set lighting and focus. Even with the lights and heaters that had been set up throughout the warehouse, it was still very cold inside. Blondie was getting cold as we stood around talking, so I opened the top of my coat and let him crawl inside to soak up some of my body heat (I really did get over my heebie-jeebies). Once he'd warmed up a bit, I felt him turn around so that his head could pop out of my coat and he could look around. The rats and I had only been in Montreal for three days, at that point, and the girl had only been their main attendant for the previous two days. She walked onto set and stood across from me, in the loose semi-circle we were talking in. She hadn't spoken and was about ten feet from me. Within a few seconds of her arrival, Blondie had crawled out of my coat and was straining toward her, obviously saying, "Take me!" in much the same way an infant will hold out its arms when it wants its mother to pick it up. The girl spotted the rat's communication and reacted without thought. It scrambled into her hands, up her arms, and into her warm coat, as if it had been doing this kind of thing all its life.

The first scene we shot put the star rats to the test right off the start. They had to run along a beam eight feet off the ground, turn a corner at an intersection, and then jump onto a fluorescent light fixture. From there, they had to jump onto the victim and appear to start eating on him!

In preparation for the scene, the production company commissioned a dummy that looked like the actor. At the last minute they thought they'd switch the real guy out and have the rats crawl around on the dummy. As luck would have it, the actor witnessed the exchange between Blonde and the girl. The affection the rat had for the girl was apparent to everyone. The actor had never been around rats before, but was quick to warm up to them. It wasn't long before he had a couple stuffed in his coat and was smiling at their antics.

They didn't need to use the dummy.

For the shot, we put our remote "clickers" along the path the rats would take, set up handlers to release them from their starting points, and waited for "Lights! Camera! Action!" It was silly to be so proud of a bunch of retired breeding rats. But, they were amazing little pro's as they cruised along the beams, doing their parts. They'd come so far in so little time. Their first <u>take</u> was a keeper.

Good timing affects how we communicate commands to our animals, but also how they perceive our intentions, moods, and desires.

Every contact we have with them tells them something about us: when we touch or don't touch them, when we say good or no, when we call them to us or tell them to go away, when we discipline them or play with them. The better timing and language skills we demonstrate the more confident and in control we are perceived as being, from our dogs point of view, and even other human beings.

Gerry called one time, to see if I'd come help on a wolf movie he had been asked to do. He told me he was busy working on a different show with his bears, and needed someone to work on a couple of the young wolves that would be on the wolf movie. He said his regular trainers were having a little trouble with them. When I asked him what was wrong, he chuckled and said, "You'll see."

The day I arrived, Gerry had the wolf handlers bring out the two pups we would be using. He stayed in the office, while I went out to meet the team I'd be leading for the next three months.

One of the crew was long time animal wrangler, master

falconer,friend and mentor, Lee Solenberger. Lee was in his late fifties or early sixties, lean and sun-weathered, a Californian Marlboro man sorta fella. Lee and I had worked on many projects and we always enjoyed some good banter. We worked well together because Lee was a master at figuring out how to rig things with the animals, when I couldn't, or didn't have the time to train them.

Like Gerry, he knew what I was about to "see" and distanced himself from the young trainers who had raised the two one-year old wolf pups. First, I asked them to show me how their animals stood on a mark. That was when I saw why Gerry had called me. In retrospect, it was really funny. Within ten seconds I could see the obstacles we had to overcome, how the problem had been caused, and the solution, which was where the haha's stopped.

The girls, who had raised the wolves, had only ever observed seasoned trainers, working trained wolves. They had attempted to imitate, and train their wolves to 'go to your mark' (a pedestal or large block big enough for the animal to stand on). The animal is supposed to go to the 'mark' and stand on it, while facing the trainer. At which point, trained wolves are thrown a piece of meat that they catch as a reward. When the year old pups were asked to go to their marks, they ran over to their pedestals and started a choreographed, frantic looking dance. They'd bounce up onto the mark, then down to the ground, up on the mark, down to the ground, up and down, up and down. They did it so fast, it made me dizzy to watch!

The girls had mixed up the steps in their training

progression. They had not understood the importance of correctly timing their rewards to bridge the gap between, what they were asking the wolves to do, and their desired action. It all snowballed, to result in mass confusion and a wonky wolf-dance routine.

I had the girls stop their wolves and stood thinking for a few seconds, with my new team watching.

Lee chewed on the corner of his handlebar moustache for a while, then in his best Southern Californian drawl asked, "Whatcha' gonna do Jackson?" Lee was good at rigging, because ropes and cables, tape and wires, are tangible objects that follow 'rules': a six foot rope is a six foot rope, if it's tied to a tree you can be pretty sure it'll stay there.

With Lee and I, my complimentary skill was the realm of rules, dictated by the animals we were working. Understanding how their minds perceived and reacted to different stimuli. Complimentary skills often present conflicting opinions. I knew Lee well enough to predict that, how I was planning to fix our dancing-wolf problem would go over, with him, like a lead balloon.

I smiled at him and said, "Just a sec," then went back into the office.

Gerry looked up from his desk with mischief and a question in his eye. In the film animal training business, it's an unspoken, ego thing, that if you have to 'ask' how to train something, you shouldn't be doing the job. With that in mind, I asked him, "Is there any reason why you don't feed your wolves by hand?"

"Nope" he answered.

I went back to the wolves... and Lee.

When I told Lee what I was planning, it was like watching a tall version of Yosemite Sam, boiling up to pitch a fit over something Bugs Bunny had done to piss him off.

Lee hollered, "YOU CAN'T FEED THOSE WOLVES BY HAND!" He stomped his feet and beat the air. He got himself pretty wound up, I knew enough to just let him rant for a bit.

After a while I said, "Alright, if I'm going to get bit, we might as well do it right. Lee can you bring out Comanche?" Comanche was a three year old wolf who would play a minor role in the film, but who hadn't fully learned a 'Mark' command. Up until that day, I had never considered hand feeding any of the wolves. From an early age, their drive for food is over-powering, they snap and guzzle food down with a vengeance, and with sharp teeth that only a fool would put their hands near. They come by their nickname of "Land Sharks" quite honestly.

Lee arrived with the test 'candidate' on a lead. He didn't spare any words letting me know that he thought I'd lost a few marbles, since the last time we'd worked together. He was worried that I was about to get chomped. I won't try to tell you that I didn't have a few misgivings as well. One of the most telling differences between domestic canines and wolves, is the size of their teeth, from their canine teeth to their molars wolves are equipped for the business they're in. My hope was in the knowledge that the wolves would just want the food, not a bite of me, and that as long as when I presented the food for them to take from my hand, I didn't move a muscle, there shouldn't be a problem.

I selected a small piece of turkey and placed it in the palm of my hand. I asked the wolf to "Mark".

As soon as his feet landed on their spot, I stepped in and offered the wolf my hand, palm up, with the treat covered by my curled fingers. As my hand neared his mouth I uncurled my fingers, exposing the meat to the wolf's tongue. I knew I couldn't move until the meat was gone. I willed myself to freeze while the wolf opened his mouth and took my hand into it. His tongue and teeth worked together, and peeled the sticky turkey off my hand and down his throat.

Whew! I'd been right, the last thing he wanted to do was bite or hurt me.

I stepped back from the wolf and showed the crew my unscathed hand. Lee grinned and shook his head in disbelief. Before he could call me 'lucky', I repeated what I had just done four or five times, again showing them that I hadn't been bitten. The timid wolf wasn't at all taken aback by having food shoved in his mouth. In some ways,

I think he preferred it. With the other wolves close by he didn't have to scramble to catch the treat, for fear of one of the others getting it first.

I lectured the crew that the trick to hand-feeding the wolves, was in the timing of the delivery, and being committed to getting the food into the animal's mouth, not just holding it out for them to 'snap at.' The more visible the meat was, the more 'snappy' the animals. So it was important to keep the meat covered until practically in their mouths. I alleviated Old Lee's fears and concerns by repeating the process with each of the wolves we'd be using.

Then one of the girls, who'd raised a wolf pup, said she wanted to try. I reviewed the actions and the philosophy behind safe hand feeding with her, warned her that if she moved she'd get bitten. Having "Seen it be done." she dismissed my advice and warnings, and with bravado, stepped up to her wolf with a chunk of turkey in hand. She told the wolf to "Mark". When he did, she stepped in to try her first 'hand-feed.' Her timing was thrown off by her fears. She lost her commitment and, as the wolf opened his mouth, she flinched. Her arm pulled back instinctively, just a little. The wolf, in the middle of pening his mouth for the treat then had to chase the food she'd offered him. Instinctually he 'caught' it - putting a canine tooth through her hand in the process. She was a tenacious girl, and in spite of the hole in her hand, eventually mastered hand feeding wolves.

Once we had them eating from our hands, it was a

simple matter of rewarding the wolves when they were <u>where</u> we wanted them to be, and so were able to overcome the crazy wolf-dance routine they had developed. In what was then believed to be a precedent, we ultimately had the young actor hand feeding the wolf on-screen.

Timing, expressed within our actions and words, creates fluidity or rhythm. To "go with the flow" and steer, is easier than trying to paddle upstream.

Rhythm

<u>Rhythm is the result of one or more actions, correctly timed, to produce a desired effect</u>.

To get going really high on a playground swing-set, several actions need to be properly timed: legs kick, arms pull, and body leans. These separate actions, timed in sync, form a rhythm that, when properly executed, sends us arcing skyward.

From longer days in summer, to seasonal breeding times or migrations, every organism on earth is influenced by or relies upon rhythms in some way.

Awareness of rhythm helps to amalgamate the parts of communication that rely on timing for their clarity. Rhythmic speech patterns are easier to understand than halting, out of time oration. Many of us have experienced the challenge of trying to understand a foreign language speaker trying to communicate in our language. Often, the most confusing part of deciphering their attempts at speaking a new language is the difference in cadence and inflection, that carries over from their native tongue. The staccato, fast paced rhythm, of middle-eastern and asian accents, requires practise for western ears to become familiar with. In North America, a long southern drawl can be confounding, to ears that are accustomed to the more clipped accents of northern latitude speakers of the same language.

Non-verbal communication is just as dependant on rhythm as the spoken word. Social animals' body language can be viewed as one language with different "Accents". These accents can vary between species, as much as the spoken word does in humans. Predator and prey animals of social species share similar facial expressions and body language, but there can be huge differences in the timing, tone, and rhythm, of how each species broadcasts a similar message.

In order to communicate clearly we need to follow prescribed rhythms for the species we're chatting with.

Pressure

Monty Roberts, horse trainer, author, and motivational speaker, popularized the phrase "Into-Pressure" animal, in his book The Man Who Listens To Horses (1999). Horses are excellent examples of how many animals respond to real or perceived "Pressures." Roberts demonstrated how horses' natural response to a predator (pressure), is to flee to a safe distance, then turn and face the threat. He showed that by using this response to pressure, we can stack the deck against a fearful horse. By using proper communication skills, we can help re-wire the horse's natural aversion to humans (predators) in a very short time.

Allowing horses to make the decision, Roberts calls, to "Join-up." Join-up, means the animal makes the decision to join or follow the human 'herd', as an alternative to remaining isolated and vulnerable. Once "Join-up" occurs it's mere moments before the horse will allow the man to climb up on his back, the same spot a mountain lion would land during an attack. In moments, the horse's perception can be altered from one extreme to the next: from the impending doom of being cornered and captured by a <u>Predator</u>, to relinquishing control and receiving comfort from the same being that it now views in a completely different light.

This susceptibility, in social species animals, is like an organic based computer glitch. This 'glitch' is a valuable tool we can use to change a social animal's perspective of us, from fear and mistrust, into love and faith, giving us control under a myriad of circumstances.

The speed of 'join-up' is affected by the animal's own experiences. Roberts made a BBC documentary
that showed his method, in practise, on a <u>wild</u> mustang separated from its herd on the open plains. Within a short time the horse stopped running, from the strange horse

with the scary rider, to 'join-up' with the new herd.

The less human association the horse has had, the quicker it seems to come around and chose to join-up with the human. Fear seems to be the catalyst in this. Once the animal's greatest fears are faced the lesser ones fall away as well.

Horses raised as pets by inexperienced horse owners, tend to lose most of their instinctual fears and can take on some dangerous behaviours, if left unchecked. Exactly the same way spoiled dogs can become lethal.

This last statement by no means, advocates the use of 'fear' or compulsion style training, but rather highlights the innate quality, and the role, fear plays in altering perspectives and developing relationships.

In the first story of this book, Porter was afraid that I was going to physically force him to comply, because that's what all the others had tried to do before. When he felt 'pressure' from the scary floating dinosaur, and I rescued him from it by 'attacking the beast', he was given the choice to either: fight me, keep running, as he had been for the last six months, or join-up with me. His choice, to offer me a play-bow and be my friend, was the 'least' scary option he had and he took it. That changed his life immeasurably, in minutes. The event also permanently altered his perception of me. He would never again need or feel, entitled to challenge me. His early upbringing had mollified any instinctual fears he had of humans. It also delayed his rehabilitation, and required a lucky and unique occasion to give him the opportunity to change his mind.

Pressure can come in a myriad of forms. From real physical pressure - like a dog pulling on a leash, to the pressure we feel from someone's look. It can be as subtle as someone invading our space by standing too close, or as overt as pushing down on a dog's bum to make it sit. In each instance, the pressure is subconsciously perceived and reacted to, before we are even conscious of it being there.

Being 'Into-pressure' is another one of those things that has flowed into our modern world from the ancient past. Developed in long extinct animals, but still surviving in today's social species animals. In short, 'Into-pressure' means: when pushed - Push back. If you throw one piece of bread into the middle of a flock of chickens, the one that pushes 'Into-pressure' the best, is most likely going to be the chicken that eats the bread.

In this discussion, pressure can be either a positive; a dog pushing its head into the hand that is petting it, or a negative; a horse pushing you up against a wall, as you try to squeeze past it in a standing stall. From elephants to schools of fish; herd behaviour is pressure sensitive.

In the mid 90's, we dropped ten goldfish into our derelict swimming pool. Within a couple years, the ten goldfish had multiplied into thousands. They were everywhere, and beautiful to watch. However, the pool was too large. The fish were shy. Whenever we tried to watch them, they'd disappear into the murky depths. It took us awhile to figure out that we weren't their only visitors. The blue herons liked watching them too, and they had quickly culled out the dimwits in the school. As a result, the rest were leery of anything above the water surface.

To tame them, we encouraged the kids to hand feed the fish. At first, we acclimatized them to eating with us standing by the pool. Then, we teased them by dropping just a few pellets into the water, with our hands hovering above the surface. Eventually, we switched to bread, and dunked our hands in the water. We then waited for the fish to nibble at the exposed pieces. Once they got used to eating from our hands, it was a simple matter of turning our hands inward and gently pushing the fish away. The 'pressure' of pushing them away from the food kicked in their 'Into-pressure', and they became the pushiest goldfish you ever saw! After a few days you couldn't put your hand in the water for more than a couple seconds, before they'd be bumping into you checking to see what goodies we had. A little twist on playing "hard to get".

Knowing how an animal will react to different types of pressures, allows us a greater degree of success when trying to predict or understand their behaviours. We also have to be aware of our role in applying and releasing pressure. Little things, like where we position ourselves in a area, can affect how the animal will move through it.

Using pressure and release of pressure as part of a communication can be tremendously effective. A dog pacing through the living room, can often be stopped by a sharp intake of breath and a hard look, the look then turned away a few 'beats' after the dog stops pacing.

For those woe-begotten chronic leash pullers, the solution is much the same except with less obvious (to the dog) input from the human.

The end to most leash-pulling problems is a simple matter of teaching people the proper perspective of what a leash is for, and how it should be used. My favourite analogy is that leashes should be seen as a version of the old safety straps used to fasten downhill skis to a skier's legs. These were used before the advent of todays brakes that pop out of the binding when a skier falls and stops the ski from sliding off down the hill unchecked.

Like the old safety straps, if your leash is tight, you've fallen and are sliding down the hill. In other words, your dog is out of control.

A leash should be viewed as a last-ditch safety strap that keeps your dog from buggering off into traffic, or chasing after the squirrel nattering at it from the base of a tree. A *tight* leash should be a 'bell' that rings, saying to us that we've got more work to do.

The steps involved in stopping leash-pulling are directly related to Timing, and how our animals are affected by feeling Pressure. The simple rule of thumb to follow is that, if you Feel pressure on the leash, you have half a second to pull it toward you, and then return your hand

and leash to its original, relaxed position. No human/dog interaction is required. What we want the dog to do is to blame the leash, for pulling on him whenever he gets too far from you. If your timing is good, and your reaction to the pressure on the leash is fast enough, the dog will quickly understand that he can walk 'at ease' as long as he doesn't get too far away from you.

Additional things to keep in mind for this exercise are, that we want the dog to figure out the size of the circle it has to work within. We are the pivot and for now, the dog is free to go full circle around us, as long as the leash is slack. To help with this, put your hand in the leash's handle, and nowhere else on the leash. Many people have a tendency to 'choke-up' on the leash, shortening the radius of the dog's circle. This adds confusion, and lengthens the amount of time required for the dog to 'get it.'

When you start out - walk slowly! We want to teach positioning first. Consider how the dog perceives 'Going for a walk.' In their world there are only three reasons to go anywhere:
  1. To eat, hunt, or drink
  2. To increase territory size
  3. To find mating partners

Two out of the three reasons to go for a walk kinda suck! Or rather, are prone to dangers. Married readers might say 3 for 3! To make a safe assumption, most of our dogs are happy to come along with us, with them assuming we're on a hunt for some kind of food!

* * *

If we follow that train of thought, look at how our dogs will behave depending on the pressures we put on them through the leash, and the speed we walk. It's easy to see how a fast moving dog might feel like it's close to having to pounce on some unknown meal, very soon. Whereas, a dog that is moving slowly has an easier time guessing that their two-legged hunting partner is just 'stalking', and hasn't targeted supper yet. Animals, 'nearing' a kill, enter a highly emotional state. High emotions make us 'stupid'!

If we make the dog check its speed with ours, give it clear signals by pulling any tension out of the leash within a half second of it starting, then returning to a pressure free leash position, our dog's leash-pulling problems are 90% solved. The remaining 10% would be those times where a distraction pulls the dog toward it, reigniting the 'Into-pressure' cycle.

In these distracted scenarios, we need to ensure we've covered all our bases on 'being the mom', have convinced our dogs that we own everything, and can start and stop everything. This latter stage can take a while to achieve, but an immediate 90% improvement in leash behaviour is better than none. A good start is a good sign!

As trainers we can use timing and pressure, in response to the information the animal is providing, to guide the animal's mind and body through new situations. Being able to over-ride one instinct (fear), with a different emotion, is crucial to attaining full, natural, control of our animals. By knowing their 'needs' we can devise pressures, to motivate them towards actions or behaviours, as if providing for their 'needs' were philosophical 'treats.'

Rue

As a young pup, Rue, a Belgian shepherd, had been orphaned and was 'farm-raised' amongst an ever changing group of visiting dogs. He was a high energy dog, and loved to wrestle and play with any creature that would have him. When I wanted to play with him, I'd initiate it by reaching over his back and grabbing his shoulder with my hand, in imitation of a gentle bite. He would respond by reaching back and putting his mouth over my wrist. We'd let go of each other, and then the fun would begin! He was quicker than most dogs. He'd spin and come back, drop into a play bow, and wait for my next move. His whole body expressed the joy he felt from having my attention. He quivered with anticipation of the rough and tumble to come, his "Party Time!"

He'd spent most of his time on the farm. When he was around seven months old, I realized his confidence off the farm wasn't what it was at home. I took him to town with me, to give him a little exposure.

As luck would have it, it was the weekend of the summer fair. The streets had been blocked off and stalls were set up, offering local produce and wares. Music blared from a bandstand in the town centre, and a large group of people enjoyed the festivities.

Culture shock for Rue, to be sure. As we approached

the crowd his excitement grew. He'd met as many people as dogs, and had loved all of them. This big gathering held the promise of more fun than he'd had in his whole life! When we walked through the not-so-crowded fringes of the group, his nose went into overdrive, trying to get a sniff of every set of legs we went by. When we passed a couple sets of people without stopping, he looked up at me with the start of a question on his face.

The next clump of people we approached drew his attention off me, and he stretched his neck out to get a whiff of a long coat we were nearing. Attached to the coat was a bossy little Pomeranian cross, with wild hair and a glittery leash. It appeared from underneath the hem of the coat, and came at Rue with all the vengeance of a swarm of hornets. He looked down at it in surprise and jumped away, putting himself on the far side of me, away from the little thing's ranting.

A few steps past the Pom, Rue looked up at me. All his excitement had faded, and a look of worry was on his face. He was sticking pretty close to my side, and had stopped poking his nose toward every new person. His tail was low and his ears were back. His hackles weren't up, but his pupils were more dilated than the sunny day dictated they should be. My wee pup was scared.

Instead of trying to comfort or reassure him, which would have translated to him as: "Yes, something is wrong in Dodge, compadre", I reached down and grabbed his shoulder, cueing him that it was time to play.

* * *

132

He automatically reached back and took my wrist in his mouth. He held it for a second then dropped it, so much as to say "Hey! Wait a minute! Here? You want to play now?"

I smiled at him and kept walking. His tail went up a bit higher, his ears perked up, and his nose started to explore again - until the next little Fru-fru popped out from behind a set of legs.

I had to 'pretend' I wanted to play with Rue a couple more times, when dogs popped out and scared him, but he succeeded in a complete loop through the down-town crowd, without a hiccup. His confidence intact and his first experience in a crowd filed away as a positive experience.

Rue took my word that the scary little dogs could pop out at any time, but they were nothing to worry about, and we were perfectly safe and fine in this big crowd. A young dog in this kind of situation, is prone to over-stimulation and extreme emotions. Being able to use a simple 'cue', that he related to his favourite game, was all that he needed to keep his brain and emotions in check. The play 'cue' gave him an option; stay scared, or play. Letting him 'choose' between two options, took his mind off of the commotion around him. His having to 'think' about playing, reduced his level of emotion and increased the likelihood that he would react in an appropriate fashion, and he did. He watched my expressions and took my cue for play as a sign that, in spite of the complete foreignness of the environment, and the threatening little dogs, all was well.

In Rue's case, the perceived pressure he felt from the crowd and small dogs was minimized by the physical pressure, when I touched his shoulder and gave the cue for him to play. Rue's perspective of me was wholesome, and he didn't have any questions about my role as his 'Mom.' In order to use pressure as part of our communication skills, it's paramount that the dog's perspective be crystal clear, in our role as the mother figure.

An animal's response to pressure can vary tremendously, and must be approached with caution. Adult animals, pressured in a negative fashion, or who perceive a real or implied "Imminent Threat", are going to react in a way that most likely ensures their own survival. Put in plain ol' English: They'll bite first, ask questions later.

The Grand Dam of survival skills is the fight-or-flight instinct. This response to danger is present and ineradicable in most mammalian life forms. Imagine the animal as a ship; the Brain as the Control Room, and Conscious Thought as the Captain. Instincts like Fight, Flight, and Freeze, would be the pilots who trade off and 'steer' the ship, when the Captain is not on the Bridge.

Imagine sneaking up on a night-shift janitor, in the wee hours of the morning, while he's bent over scrubbing out a toilet in a dimly lit stall. If you're quiet and get right behind him, stretch out your hands to either side of his rib cage, GRAB him and roar "Aaaaarrgh"! Would you be surprised if, seconds later, you wound up with a toilet brush protruding from a cranial orifice?

In this same way, a dog's reactions to extreme pressure, perceived or real, should be anticipated and, if or when they occur, acknowledged as the reflex action that they are, rather than as a character flaw or dangerous animal designation. A thorough understanding of our dog's limitations allows us to know at what point the imaginary line is crossed, that puts them into reflexive action.

Pressure can be applied through visual, auditory, and sensory means. It's critical, for safety sake, that all of the earlier steps of emotional control, ownership, and perspective, be in place before experimenting with varying pressures. Working with adult dogs in this fashion can be precarious, if the proper progressions are not followed.

Sabre taught me that lesson one morning at the SPCA shelter, where I'd worked for years. He was a magnificent five year old Rottweiler who had been surrendered, because of dog-dog aggression his owners were unable to deal with. When no other dogs were around, he was a wonderful example of the big breed. But with other dogs in sight, he was an obsessed menace.

I'd spent a little time with him, over a few days, and on that morning had listened to a co-worker tell about a 'revolutionary' new distraction technique. The theory seemed to hold some merit, so I thought Sabre would be a good guy to experiment on.

I'd placed a little old grumpy Rottie-cross we'd had in for months, in a side pen and used him as bait to get Sabre wound up. The little dog couldn't have cared less about Sabre's ranting. To say the least, the set up worked well, but the new distraction technique failed.

Sabre was in full-on "Hate" mode, when I gave up on the theory we'd decided to try on for size.

Instead, I went to a compulsion based correction. I knew better, but was feeling lazy, and hurried to finish up with Sabre and carry on with the rest of the morning chores. I had knelt beside him at the start, but he'd turned his back to me, when he squared off to bark and threaten the dog in the pen, about fifty feet away from us. Sabre had worked himself into a state of heightened emotions. I made the mistake of trying to 'correct him' out of it. The other mistake I made was I hadn't established myself well enough, as a "mother" or leader of any kind, in Sabre's eyes. When I told him to "Stop", by touching his loin with rigid fingers and firm pressure, he turned his head over his shoulder and gave me the 'Look', he then turned back to holler at the little Rottie-cross some more. The second time I told him to "Stop", he looked back with the eye and growled at me. Then back to Rottie-cross taunting.

Now, anyone in their right mind would have led the dog away and started from a better place. But no, not me! I had gone right along with Sabre! Heightened emotions had made me stupid, too. So I gave him his third order to "Stop".

* * *

He wheeled around fast, with his mouth wide open. I was on my knees so his teeth were coming right at my face. I grabbed him under the neck with my left hand, and turned with him as he came at me, rising to my feet at the same time. His momentum powered the arch he made. I guided his head upwards, past my head, until his feet left the ground. Then I laid him down on the ground on his back. I landed on top, straddling him, my left hand firmly holding the thick hide of his neck. He fought to get me off. He kicked with all four legs and unbalanced me, causing me to roll forward over top his head. With my right hand, I reached for the ground to stop myself. As it went past Sabre's face, he tried to bite it and missed. I caught myself, and repositioned my weight over top of him and sat up. He was still struggling against my left hand. I brought my right hand back over top his head and left it just out of his reach, waiting. Working with predators, you're taught that if the worst thing happens and you're going to get bit, shove your hand down their throat.

I had learned the value of that lesson many times. As someone who dealt predominantly with aggressive dogs, I had had many occasions to use it, both as self-defence, and on over rambunctious pups who liked to play-bite too hard. Predators' reaction to having something shoved in to the back of their mouths is universal. The mouth opens up, and they turn away and try to clear their airway. The effect is like a tripped electrical breaker that will only reset after the object is removed from the back of the mouth. The molars will scratch the hell out of you, and you'll bleed a bit, but it's a better alternative to being severely chomped on.

With Sabre fighting underneath me I felt the need to use this trick. The only other alternative, I had at the time, was to physically carry him back to his kennel and close the door, to avoid being bit.

Sabre didn't care what tricks I knew. He just wanted me to let him up, so he could finish me off and get back to the little Rottie that had pissed him off in the first place.

Being left-handed I was used to making the grab for the neck with my right hand, keeping my left free for all the important stuff, like tickling dog tonsils (do they have tonsils?). But alas, grabbing with an untrained hand, I had failed to adjust. Little did I know at the time, my left hand had caught Sabre at mid-neck. I hadn't noticed it wasn't up under his jawline, where it should have been, to pin his head so that he couldn't move it off the ground. Sabre lay straining against me with his legs, and wriggled onto his back.

I took a breath, waiting for him to bite again. My right hand was just inches above his black and tan face that was full of rage.

In what seemed like slow motion. I watch him lift his head off the ground. A fleeting thought saw the movement and mentioned "that's not supposed to be happening". His mouth opened, and before I could turn my right hand and put it down the back of his mouth, he sunk a canine tooth between my middle and index fingers, above the knuckles, just one chomp. Once he'd made his point, he let go and put his head back down on the ground, pushing harder with his legs. My hand had a little purple hole in it, with a thin bit of torn tendon dangling from it.

"He got me!" was all my constricted brain could inform me about what had just happened.

Self-preservation kicked in next, and I realized that I needed to figure out Plan B. I wasn't used to having to go to Plan B!

I wound up carrying Sabre, still fighting, into the kennel and dropped him into his cage and closed the door.

I'd been working animals for decades, had been helping with the homeless dogs in our shelter for almost ten years, and I'd never been really 'bitten'. After a quick trip into town for a little first-aid, I went back to work, embarrassed that I'd finally been nailed.

The manager was waiting for me. She'd heard what had happened, and when I returned, she announced that she wanted Sabre euthanized. I said, "Don't you dare! I asked for everything I got. He's all right. I'm the one who screwed up." And I had, severely.

Sabre and I patched up our differences, and he was eventually re-homed safely, without fear of further incidents. He would always be a dog that would only take so much 'pressure', but he was bid-able and, with his new confident owner who understood him, he relinquished his tough guy role for that of a big goofy Rottie.

Had I taken the time with Sabre that he required, in order to develop a proper bond and perspective of me, it's likely that he would never have considered biting, under any situation. I pushed him too hard, at the wrong time. I paid the price, and re-learning a lesson I'd learned the hard way many times before. Another abiding Therrien-ism applies: "*The only thing we "get" from being in a rush with animals - is getting something hurt.*"

Too many dogs are euthanized every year, because of this kind of error, made by unknowing dog owners who, like me, got in a rush and wound up 'hurting something.'

Owners often miss seeing the source of pressure that influences their dogs. It's easy to miss their signals of unease or distress, if they are behind us, or if we're not watching with our peripheral vision. The common scenario of dogs and people, meeting on a hiking trail, is a familiar example for people to relate to in this regard.

In this situation, people often pull their dogs in closer to themselves, making room for the approaching people to pass. The dog, who is also focussed on the on-coming traffic feels <u>implied</u> <u>pressure</u> coming from the strangers. When the leash is tightened, the implied pressure manifests as a physical one in the dog's mind and blame is directed toward the strange dog. This sets the stage for the all too common 'Blazing guns at ten paces'.

Having alternative, 'positive' pressures or cues, that can

be applied to counteract rising emotions, or perceived pressures, is a handy, multipurpose tool to have in any animal relationship. Understanding these pressure options allows us to temper experiences or avoid environments that our animals might not be prepared to meet. Understanding how pressure works with our animals is a foundation concept that is essential to realizing authentic communication skills. It can help with the development of strong bonds and increased trust levels.

Whether we use physical or implied pressure, the use of good timing and rhythm makes all the difference. When we apply 'pressure,' as in giving a command or pulling on the leash, the follow-through must result in the animal feeling the release of pressure. If the animal fails to feel a release from the pressure (real or imagined), it will more likely behave from its instinctual base and forget all the good stuff that we've taught it. In short, if we put pressure on and don't take it off - the animal spends it's mental resources focussed on: the pressure, its cause and how to react to or avoid it; instead of focussing on us, so we can lead it in the direction we want things to go.

The more intense a pressure is perceived by the dog, the deeper into the limbic system its mind is pushed. With an animal operating from that region of the brain we can count on them being only one thing - "stupid."

We just need to look at our own reactions to pressure to be able to relate. If someone pushes against us, our limbic system filters through the information our senses input and sets off the appropriate alarms. Depending on the environment, the force and duration of the push and who is pushing us, we can experience a wide range of reflex actions and emotions (try it out with a partner!). It is harder to regain normal thought processes while the pressure is still being applied. Hence the necessity of releasing pressure in a timely fashion when it is being applied to our animals.

In everyday training or communications the rhythm of appropriate pressure use should become practised and fluid. Pressure on. Pressure off. Pause.

Pressure on: a verbal/hand cue with eye contact.

Pressure off: eye contact shifts to a more peripheral gaze and the hand cue is frozen or removed.

Pause: stillness, static pressure waiting for the dog's response.

The pause is when the golden moments can occur. The pause gives the animal the opportunity to think about what the pressure meant and how it should respond. The length of the pause depends on the animals reaction. Some will think hard and take a few seconds to decide and then act, others quickly forget and think about something else.

Knowing the animal's personality will help us time, when to start repeating the Pressure on - Pressure off process. Depending on the situation we can decide to increase or decrease the pressure to further encourage our animals. Pressure can be a positive or a negative and knowing how to balance pressure takes practise.

A dog that has a high food drive can get 'stupid' if we try to work them with food and *show* them too much of the treat, or if we hold the food too close to their noses.

A timid dog can be made 'stupid' if we use exaggerated hand cues with too strong eye contact or over loud voice commands.

Keeping our dogs in their *right minds* by using balanced pressure and avoiding them running on their limbic systems is essential.

Tone

Q: Why do Shepherds use whistles to direct their border collies?
A: Whistle's don't carry "tone"

Q: Why won't your dog come to you when you call him, after you find the garbage torn open for the second time in a day?
A: Voices carry "tone"

"Tone of voice" is the first thing that pops to mind when the subject is brought up during sessions. But when clients are given a few quick facial expressions as examples, they see how tone is involved with more than just spoken language.

The 'Tone' we use for communicating our thoughts and feelings, conveys significant weight and meaning to our audience. Body language, facial expressions, and other nonverbal facets, are injected with <u>tone</u>. The speed that we move our hands when gesturing, the muscle tension involved in a grimace, or the exaggeration of a <u>look</u>, all tell the receiver the degree or tone, of the emotion that is implied in the expression.

The tone of our voice is translated by our dogs on a simple scale:

Low vocal tones: carry sentiments of confidence, threat, or resolve. (Picture: Big Tough Dude)
High vocal tones: convey insecurity, fear, excitement, or pain. (Picture: Little Sucky Wimp)

If we consider the number of ways we can confuse our dogs on a daily basis, just by talking to them, it's surprising there aren't more dog psych-wards for the permanently insane. Here's a fictional scenario to demonstrate.

Jill comes home after a hard day's work. She's a young woman raised in a city, and remembers her only childhood pet as a vague memory. It had been a small dog that she had been very close too. She'd loved dressing it up, and pulling it around their cul-de-sac in a bright red wagon.

As an adult out on her own, Jill wanted to do her part

to make a difference in the world. She rescued a couple of homeless dogs from a local shelter and lavished them with every recommended food, toy, or treatment. She was sensitive to their sad histories, and did her best to avoid dredging up bad memories. The smallest one had been terrorized by a school aged group of young boys. The bigger dog had been abandoned and found running loose, emaciated, and suffering a chronic skin infection.

She could hear their welcoming chorus, from inside the house, as she exited her car with the groceries she'd rushed in to get on her way home. She pushed back the dogs, as she opened the door, dropped a big bag of dog food on the floor, and set a little bag of pre-made salad on the counter. Toenails clicked a staccato fanfare, in honour of her arrival. The dogs' noses bumped her legs, crowding her in the entryway. Jill is just as happy to see them as they are to see her.

"Oh My B-a-a-BIES! She squealed to them, dropped to her knees, and embraced the excited pair. A blur of wet tongues, petting hands, and wagging tails culminated in Jill becoming the filling for a human-sandwich.

From all appearances, especially the happy dog's warm greeting display, the above story depicts a happy home and an owner who is beyond reproach, in her style of dog-care.

Until we turn the story around and look at it from the dog's perspective...

* * *

Their fearless mother leaves and hunts ALONE all day long, then comes home with an amazing amount of bounty. Her dogs idolize her, but then their fearless huntress takes on a submissive role...

Jill's, "Oh My B-a-a-aBIES!" Sounds to their ears like an over excited pup about to submissively pee all over the floor, doing all she can to convince the "Adults" that she's still a puppy.

Jill, dropping to the ground for a good-lovin' session, also carries potentially confusing signs to her dogs. Their real mothers would never have tolerated them bowling her over, during a greeting display, but Jill obviously enjoys it so they continue and are encouraged even further.

It's hard for dog owners to identify the consequences possible, in this kind of scenario, mainly because the side-effects of the confusion, Jill's dogs' experience, may only be visible in a completely different environment.

When Jill takes her dogs for a walk, the dog's confusion can manifest as symptoms of doubt in her capacity to keep them all safe, against other dogs, or possibly even people they meet in the neutral 'territories' their walks lead them through. Their doubt in her can create, insecurities and increase innate fears of strange animals, which produces an elevated likelihood that they will take on a more dominant appearing role: barking to warn away strange dogs, threatening people, or responding poorly to Jill's commands and authority.

* * *

The way Jill could have helped avert the confusion in this scenario is by slightly tweaking her interactions on arriving home. Imitating a mother dog returning from a hunt, is pretty easy after a long day's work!

I ask clients to envision an old Babushka carrying wood on her back down an icy windblown street, her tattered woollen dress billowing, her blue tinged legs exposed above her patched rubber boots. Her grandchildren, huddled around the fireplace, race to open the door for her and help unload her burden. Not one child daring to demand, or take, anything from her until she's shed her overcoat and settled into her rocker. Once settled, and warmed a little, her face softens and she addresses one or the other of the children; inviting them to come and sit on her lap and tell her about their day.

Next, I'll draw a parallel for them, of a tired old momma wolf who's spent the day wading through the snow to catch a measly little rabbit for her six pups.

Through their countenance, these two old mommas use the 'tone' of their body language to relate to their young that, 'Now' is not the time for foolin' around. Once settled, their tones would soften, and appropriate greetings would take place. No mad rush that could hurt tired, old backs or sore feet.

I've encouraged pet owners to practise coming home and being that growly old babushka. Walk into their house with a roar that says "Leave me alone"! I ask them

147

to move slowly, set all their stuff down, make their way to a favorite chair, sit and take a few good breaths. Then, single out one dog, if they have multiples, and ask it to come over for a pet. Then I get them to end it, before their dog gets too excited, have it go back and lay down where it had been, and call another dog over.

It's not easy to do. You have to put out a really over-the-top 'evil' air to counteract their exuberance at your arrival. But giving our dogs the perspective that, 'Sometimes, Mom has to be approached with caution', can have far reaching effects on their trust in our abilities to control situations.

We keep pets to complement our existence, and to share our affections. The above dialogue should in no way, be taken as discouraging contact, affection, or playfulness. But it should remind us, once more, of our need to be the one who 'starts and stops' everything. As a means to having our animals perceive us as that all important, 'mother figure.' Affection and play are primary bonding tools. The more the better, providing it's the right kind, at the right time.

Touch

Scene 1: Her fingertips gently stroked the baby's back, while it drifted near sleep. The baby, lulled by the comforting touch of her mother's hand, went to sleep. (End Scene)

Scene 2: Her fingertips gently stroked her husband's

back, while he drifted near sleep. He was comforted by her touch and could feel that she wasn't thinking of sleep. (End Scene)

Oh STOP it! There is a point!

In both scenarios, the mechanics of the woman's touch was similar - but with dramatically different intents and desired responses.

At this point we start to wade into an esoteric stream. Senses like touch and smell, are so subjective they defy accurate means to compare, weigh, or measure between individuals.

The way we touch our animals can have profound effects on their behaviour and actions.

Simba

Darrel and Simba, a three year old bull mastiff, came to me troubled by the dog's uncontrollable exuberance toward people. Darrel complained that the dog would bowl people over, leave trails of slobber everywhere, and generally be a nuisance, whenever the dog took a notion to be affectionate - which was often! As a result, Simba spent much of the time alone, isolated from those he most wanted to be near. Darrel worried that his large dog was becoming a liability when his children and their friends came over to play.

Darrel told me how, as a young pup, Simba had

excelled in puppy class and, at a year old, had gone through obedience class with flying colours. He went on to explain that he had "Let things go with the Simba", during a marital split up. He felt guilty that, for much of the time following his divorce, he had been consumed by other matters and had not had time for Simba.

Simba was a big lover. He'd been brought into the family as a pup, and had only ever known the love of Darrel, his wife and two daughters, with all their games and affection. The intervening time of turmoil in the adult's break-up, destroyed the familiar environment to which he was accustomed.

When it was all changed, and he found himself alone in an empty house for most of the time, his normal levels of socialization and stimulation evaporated. When the children would come to Darrel's for the weekend, Simba was like an addict trying to soak up as much of what he'd been missing as he could. His need to compensate drove him to a frenzied state, and eventually he became the drooling, needy, monster that Darrel showed up with.

Simba was effusive with any kindly contact he received. His problem, that had started when he was ignored, had grown out of control. His patience and manners were poor. He had to be the centre of attention. If nobody would do it, he'd pet himself, by rubbing up against whichever person he happened to take a fancy to at the moment. No one corrected his behaviour, except to isolate him in the yard or his kennel.

* * *

In short, he appeared to be a big spoiled pup looking for comfort.

Darrel was right when he had guessed that their problems came from his inattention to the dog, and for letting things go.

Simba's behaviour stemmed from his needs, and was rooted in positive, affectionate, intentions. Darrel wanted to learn how to correct the problem, but I cautioned him that, making a negative out of Simba's behaviour would have been tantamount to smacking a child for giving someone a much felt hug. I had an idea I wanted to try with the big guy, so I had Darrel leave him with me for a few days.

All the big dog needed was to be reminded of his manners, from when he was a pup. He'd learned that the easiest way to get the attention he wanted was by forcing himself on people. He didn't know his long strings of drool and friendly over-sized demeanour, worked against him. In the kindest way I knew how, I showed Simba a better way of getting what he wanted, without filling the washing machine with drool soaked clothes.

The solution was quick and simple.

I left him in the barn for the night.

In the morning when I opened the door I had one big, excited dog on my hands! He bounced at the end of the long-line and strained with all he had to get close to me.

Using the hand-signal Simba had learned as a pup, I stood in the doorway, about twenty feet from him, and waited for him to sit.

He whined and bounced on his front legs. He tugged on the long-line so hard I wondered for a minute, if it would hold. He bounced and whined louder. Then he barked.

I left.

I stood around the corner, just outside the barn. When he quit barking and went back to whining, I counted to three and returned to my spot in the doorway.

I kept my expressions neutral and signalled him for him to sit.

He whined, strained, and bounced again.

I stopped signalling, tilted my chin up, looked over my shoulder, and turned my head as if I were about to leave. He stopped bouncing. I looked back toward him and repeated the hand signal.

His eyes seemed to get a little bigger.

His head came up and he froze for a second. He looked at the ground in front of him, then back up at me. He whined, moved side to side a little on his front end, and then went back to pulling and bouncing.

* * *

I left.

The Third time I re-entered the barn, the big guy was ready to negotiate. His whine was quieter and he didn't tug on the line with near as much force.

I stood in the doorway, motionless for a couple seconds, until he stopped pulling altogether and milled about on the spot. He watched me, with his forehead wrinkled. This time when I raised my hand to tell him to sit, he looked at the ground in front of him again, then as he looked up at me, Simba plunked his big butt down and sat.

Hallelujah!

At the instant his bum touched the floor, I started to move toward him. Slow movements, one step at a time. While I moved, I let my arm lower to my side and turned the palm toward Simba with a distant, visual, promise of a touch on its way.

Oh he tried! His tail wagged across the floor and got his whole body vibrating. He managed to sit, until I got about ten feet from him, then he couldn't hold his bum on floor any longer. His wagging tail lifted him back to a standing position.

I left.

The next round I made it right up to him, before his bum left the ground. The time after that, he turned his face to lick my hand as I reached out to touch him. He learned that that movement made me leave too. He whined and bounced with impatience, as I left. Simba was getting really frustrated.

The next pass, I helped him out by distracting his attention with my other hand. I raised it above his head, as if I were going to pet him from above. When he focused on that hand, I pressed my other against his cheek and squeezed his thick skin with my fingers, holding my hand there, pressing back against him as hard as he pressed against me. He pushed against my hand, his eyes half closed, relishing the contact that he'd been after for the past few minutes.

His reward was short lived. When I pulled my hand away from his face with the intent of stroking his ear and neck, he couldn't help trying to say "thank you" by licking my hand.

I left.

That first contact motivated the big guy, and his slow moving bull-mastiff brain bridged the gap. He had begun to figure out that I wanted something from him, and had started to think rather than just slobbering about. At first, when he would move to lick or reciprocate affections, I would pull my hand back and give him a chance. Withdrawing anytime he would do something, or move, in a way that I hadn't asked him.

The next couple of rounds saw him sitting like a

sentinel, looking up with bright eyes, attentive and lively, while he held his body in check as I petted his head, cheeks, neck, and shoulders. Once he succeeded in accepting the slow calming strokes from me in a standing position, I bent down, bringing my face closer to his. My demeanour remained neutral, but I was teasing him. His tongue shot out of his mouth and he licked my cheek.

Yup! I left.

With incremental successes, mixed with my absence when he'd screw up, it only took about twenty minutes for us to refresh Simba's memory about appropriate contact. We walked out of the barn on a slack leash, the big slobber-puss minding his manners like a proper gentleman.

Touch and timing were all that were used in restoring his earlier levels of behaviour. Not one word was used, or needed, for Simba's benefit. He just needed to see something he could understand, and be shown how to get what he wanted the most - a gentle touch.

Visualization

The eight year old girl and her mother met me at an empty soccer field near their home. Their dog was an eight month old giant schnauzer that had been diligently raised and trained by the whole family. We'd started them off on the right foot, when the dog was eight weeks old. At eight months, when the dog hit puberty, she was as tall as the girl was and outweighed her by a fair bit. The mother called saying she was worried because the dog had begun to ignore the girl, when she tried to make it perform. So we booked a session to clear up the problem, before it got out of hand.

A short time before this, I had been fortunate to attend a talk by Dr. Alan Schoen DVM, who had just released a book discussing our pets' senses and their capacity for love. His talk ventured into some esoteric territory. It was fun! It touched on new-age philosophies, and brushed into the realm of spirituality, and other subjective venues that were compelling, but seemed impractical in dealing with the day to day dog problems with my own clients, who ranged from school aged children, to old farmers with staunch ideals. His talk was motivational, nonetheless I appreciated his courage when he addressed opinions that were scientifically ambiguous, but rooted in logic and common sense insights. Dr. Schoen is a Vet, who after years of Western medicine experience and field observations, switched to Eastern philosophy medicine as a preferred course for treating patients.

Since the lecture, I'd been wondering how I could inject my classes with some of my own unconventional beliefs. I had never thought to include these views in lessons, for lack of being able to prove their point, and for fear of sounding aerie-faerie. The little girl and her dog offered up the perfect opportunity to experiment. It's far less intimidating to have an eight year old girl question your sanity than it is to face the bewilderment of an adult, who's wondering how many bricks you've lost from your load.

As it turned out, I'll always be grateful to Dr. Schoen for leading the way to embracing the "Mystical side."

The giant schnauzer was a sweet dog. Their only complaint was her disregard for the girl's authority. The dog was tall, standing at eye level to the girl. It only took a glance to see what was happening. Their challenge was being caused by the dog's need for attention, and a 'tea-party' assumption the dog was making, that the girl was her surrogate litter-mate.

Litter-mates are to be played, snuggled, and argued with, not ordered around by, or dictated by, especially not the puny ones!

After we had said our "Hellos", I told them we were going to try something they hadn't done before. I asked the girl to take her dog out into the middle of the soccer field, have the dog lie down and stay. Then the girl was to leave the dog and stand at a distance, for a short while. I then told her that I wanted her to go back to the dog and, without pushing her, try to make the dog lay on its side with her head in the grass. I clarified to the girl once more, that she could touch the dog, but wasn't to push her to make her lay down.

"Okay. But she doesn't know how to do that." The girl said before heading off.

"I know." I assured her as she left, "I just want you to go and try it, okay?"

The first part was easy for them. The dog lay down and watched the girl move away from her. When I cued the girl to go back to the dog, she moved to the dog's head and knelt in the grass, off to one side of her. From where the girl's mother and I stood, we could see the girl pointing to the dog. Her arm movements were brisk (loud). The dog watched her contortions for a while, and then stared off across the field. Even at fifty yards it was clear what the dog was *saying* to the girl. It was dog language to the effect of: "Yeah, Yeah, Whatever! Shuddup will ya?!"

I smiled at the mother and put a finger up to say, "Just a sec", and headed across the field to the frustrated girl and her dog. She was a dedicated little student and she didn't like failing at a challenge.

When I got up to them I said, "That's okay, you did well. We knew she didn't know how to do it. So now, let's try this, okay?" She listened intently, nodding. "I want you to do the same thing all over again. Move her over a little when I tell you to, and do what you just did, again. Except this time when you go back to her, I want you to see in your head exactly what it is you want her to do - and make it come out your hand."

She looked at me as if I'd just said the most logical thing in the world! *You gotta love kids!* The girl stayed sitting beside her dog as I walked back to where her mother stood. When I'd finished the walk back, I cued her to go ahead and start over.

Life is full of those fish stories of the one that got away. Then there're those moments when we wish a video camera had been recording a rare event. This moment was one of those.

The girl brought the dog to its feet and moved it over about ten steps. Then she went through the same routine. When I cued her to go back to her dog, she walked slower than she had the first time. She stopped in front of the dog, in much the same position that she had been in on her first try. This time she paused before kneeling. It was only a second or two, but you could tell she was thinking. Her head was scrunched down between her shoulders, and she stood looking at her hands that she held out in front of her at waist height.

The next few seconds were magical! She settled herself in the grass. The dog watched her intently. We watched as the girl slowly brought her hand up from her lap and placed it on the dog's cheek. The dog rolled with the girl's touch and flopped on its side, head on the grass, doing exactly what the girl and visualized it doing.

Bewildered, the mother asked, "What did you say to her?"

From then on I've included discussions about the benefits of visualizing our dog's actions and behaviours, as a normal part of sessions. It turns out, that even today's staunch old farmers are far more open minded than I thought they would be.

Today, visualization is embraced in everything from

sports to psychotherapy. The argument goes on about how it works, but most indications are overwhelming in its positive effects. An experiment with three groups of golfers was conducted. One group was given how-to books as a resource, and another other group was to use visualization. The third group, the control group, changed nothing. The visualization group showed marked improvement in timing and rhythm, over their counterparts who'd been given the how-to books. Both improved compared to the control group.

Optimizing our own skills, prior to interfering in the lives of dogs or other animals as trainers, is only rational and fair. Being able to visualize multiple outcomes to a given scenario effectively, allows us to prepare for the best AND worst possible outcomes. Keeping everyone safe and helping to avoid the need to backtrack because of negative experiences that could have been avoided, with proper foresight.

Practice makes perfect

It's all fine and dandy to talk about something, but being able to "Walk-the-Talk is what it's all about." How to put all of the layers and pieces of language together, and have it result in better control and relationships with our animals, is where we wind up finding ourselves near the end of sessions with clients.

For clients, the how-to of better control and relations with their animals, depend on the individuals involved, their histories, and the state of their relationship. I learned a long time ago, that the trust required for someone to try speaking a foreign language, in front of a relative stranger, isn't usually acquired by the time we get to this part of the session. So I give them what I feel is the next best thing. In as many ways as possible, at the risk of appearing goofy as a loon, I speak "dog" to them, as we quickly review all the parts of non-verbal language that we've covered. I give them scenarios and act out examples of movement, posture, and expression, to give them visual and auditory examples of our topic.

My logic for doing this is simple. I don't expect them to 'learn it all' in the time we have together, and the development of their communication skills will take more than a few trials and errors. I tell them, I want them to go home and practice in a mirror, or amongst themselves, before trying it out on their dogs. Like any other animal, we humans benefit from learning through play. Enjoyable, focused, attention is a rare commodity in many people's lives. But at home, locked in our bathrooms, the mirror is a safe place to turn the little predator in us all lose, for a little bit of run-around time! Not one of us hasn't made faces in a mirror, or tried out a few 'good lines' on ourselves. It's the perfect spot to try out some old facial expressions, with a new intent before trying it on for 'real' with our pets.

Video recording, and watching our body language, is another good way to study how our movements and tone are expressed without words. It is also a good way to see how we are perceived by others.

* * *

On the film sets I've been on, I've always been surprised by how little the animals reacted to the "Acting" that goes on around them. One scene called for the dog to react as the actress let out a blood curdling scream. The dog was in place and the dog's trainer was confident the dog would respond as the director needed. So, put the dog in place and let the cameras roll. The actress's scream convinced me! But the dog, without moving his head, gave the actress a sideways glance, then looked back to his trainer as much as to say "What?! It's her not me!"

If we're going to be fluent and convincing with body language, it needs to be authentic. Practising our timing, rhythm, pressure, and tone, being aware of our touch, and using visualization to see the exact images of our dog's perfect behaviours, is a long road that, leads a straight course to our desired results.

Our own worst enemy can sometimes be ourselves. Doubt is a heavy toll that can come into play at this stage of the game. Doubting ourselves, or what we're doing, is an effective survival tool. But, when learning new skills, or refining the ones we already have, doubt can delay our progress considerably. It throws off our timing and can destroy our rhythm. For these reasons; I emphasize to all my clients that they practise reading body language and utilizing their communication skills, in the proper progression. Just as we will discuss progressions plans for training our dogs in the next chapter, we want to set up every animal in the game to succeed. This works best when the learning and perfecting of skills is done in the right order, before setting ourselves up for too big a challenge.

The Truth about Trainers

Manipulation

Fortunes have been made selling products designed to improve our "Powers of persuasion." The ancient Greeks were its earliest advocates. Schools of Rhetoric taught their students to argue both sides of an issue, in order to promote recognition of all sides of an argument. In some ways we could use a resurgence of these philosophies in today's strife filled world. Skewed perspectives make poor drivers.

When it comes to comparing animal trainers an old saying is that: If you put two of them in a room together, the only thing they will agree upon is that the other one is wrong. The one thing most exceptional animal trainers have in common is the ability to be persuasive; both with humans and their selected species of animal.

To take an honest look at the skill of Persuasion, either from an animal training point of view or from a humanistic one, we're forced to look at the "whole deal".

By way of metaphor: Persuade has a sister called Influence. They're part of the Control family. Their cousins, Manipulate and Deceit, come from the wrong side of the tracks but they're close kin.

As social species animals, humans relate to the Control

family from instinctual ties forged in long forgotten times. Our dogs, cows, horses, and other domestic animals, also have a connection with the *familia-del-Control*. Their relationship with the Control Family, as ours, is a history of long, successful ventures that bring us back, time and again, into the fruitful familiarity that comes from this clan's talents.

We should look at the 'meaning' of their names first, or their First names, if you want to continue with the metaphor.

Persuade:
1: to move by argument, entreaty, or expostulation to a belief, position, or course of action
2: to plead with: urge

Influence:
1a: an ethereal fluid held to flow from the stars and to affect the actions of humans
b: an emanation of occult power held to derive from stars
2: an emanation of spiritual or moral force
3a: the act or power of producing an effect, without apparent exertion of force or direct exercise of command
b: corrupt interference with authority for personal gain
4: the power or capacity of causing an effect in indirect or intangible ways: sway
5: one that exerts influence

Manipulate:
1: to treat or operate with, or as if with, the hands or by

mechanical means especially in a skillful manner

2a: to manage or utilize skillfully

b: to control or play upon by artful, unfair, or insidious means especially to one's own advantage

3: to change by artful or unfair means, so as to serve one's purpose: doctor

Deceit:

1: the act or practice of deceiving: deception

2: an attempt or device to deceive: trick

3: the quality of being deceitful: deceitfulness

The common trait, in these Control family members, is to provide for those inborn needs present in social animals. They are executed through various means of communication, from words to expressions, or the omission thereof. Particularly in times of heightened emotions, social animals will resort to enlisting one or more of the 'family' to accomplish or attain the resources or compliance from other beings.

Of the four Control family members, Manipulation is the umbrella that covers them all. Its manifestation can be influential and persuasive, as well as deceptive, all at the same time. Manipulation of one or more animals can be so subtle, that the signal given by the sender is visible only to the intended receiver.

A friend of mine brought her dogs over on a regular basis. One of her dogs, was a sweet little pitbull with a tragic past. In spite of it all she had attained ambassador status as an SPCA success story, going to schools for pet education lectures, and spending her days as a greeter to people, and homeless and injured animals at a shelter. She was unflappable; sweet as pie, and could do no wrong.

At the time, I had Tessa visiting while her owner was away. Tess, a Cocker Spaniel, had also had a rough start but was making good progress becoming more social and less 'snappy.' One evening, while we were watching a movie, I noticed Holly eyeing Tess from across the room. It was subtle. Holly was flopped on a couch with her head on her paws, but her ears were pulled back and lifted a bit. Her forehead had a slight wrinkle to it, and for just a second she flared her eyes while looking at Tess. Tess was perched in her bed in the bay window, across the room from Holly. Tess had been over-seeing the goings-on between the other dogs. She hadn't built up the confidence yet, to try interacting or playing with the other dogs by this point, though she would watch on with a dour look on her face.

When Holly gave her the *look*, I was lucky to have been where I could see both dogs at once. Tess reacted by 'retreating' with her head; she looked over her shoulder, away from Holly. Once Tess had hidden her eyes from her, Holly had relaxed her ears and turned her eyes back to the floor, where two of the other dogs lay. After a few beats, Tessa looked back into the room as she had been before. Again Holly, without moving her head, perked up and gave Tess the eye. Again Tess turned her head away from the rest of the room. I surprised everybody by catching Holly in her game and growled to her, "Holly, you knock it off!" My friend jumped and looked at me like

I was crazy, for giving her dog heck for lying on the couch! When I'd spoken, Holly had known what I was talking about. She'd dropped her ears and looked back at the floor instantly. When we'd started talking about what had caused my *outburst*, Holly sat up on the couch to watch. Tessa had turned to look at us too. So as not to be thought of as a weirdo, after I'd told her what'd happened, I said, "Just watch".

We stopped talking and watched the dogs. It wasn't more than a few seconds before Holly put Tessa out of the group with her 'evil-eye' again, this time from a sitting position. Tessa started to turn away from us. Then at the last second, she flicked her eyes back toward me. She saw I was watching her, and I saw her eyes flash. I was her back-up! It gave her courage. She broke her gaze with me and locked eyes with Holly. A silent bitch-fight of dirty looks broke out from across the room. I was off the hook! Holly had been caught, and Tessa was relieved of the silent intimidation she'd been experiencing. In this instance, seeking to 'blame' one dog or the other for their animosity, would have been pointless - as relevant as trying to seek out why two children on a playground don't get along. Sometimes they just don't, or won't, no matter what we do. Like personality clashes with adult human beings. The two dogs never became close 'friends', but they learned to tolerate each other's presence without continuing the silent battle they'd been caught in.

It's common to meet people with misbehaving animals. Often the people are smart, logical, and astute in human communication skills and etiquette. Yet they are over-run by their furry beast(s), who perpetrate raucous acts of disobedience and entitlement that the human would never accept from a contemporary of any age or relation. These same people often justify their dog's actions as being silly or juvenile, but based in love and therefore, they feel helpless in 'correcting' those actions that cause liability or grief on a daily basis. Often, the hellion of a dog is carrying out his own "con" job on the people. When they're shown, through demonstrations with predicted outcomes, that their dog has just been 'foolin" them, the tables can turn pretty quick!

Manipulation, as defined above: "3: <u>To change by artful... means so as to serve one's purpose</u>." can benefit us, as trainers, if we embrace this view of manipulation and bring to bear its full positive potential; from what is commonly seen as an abhorrent practise. We can achieve deeper insights and relations, resulting in better control and confidence in our animals, than if we manipulate in a negative light, under the alternative definition of: "1:<u> to treat or operate... as if with the hands or by mechanical means...</u>"

The ability to persuade or manipulate is one more of those "older than we are", instincts that we've evolved with. Knowing when we are being manipulated is also important when we're dealing with smart animals.

Before we're born, we begin practicing skills we'll need, once we get out! Ultra-sounds have captured human fetuses in the act of everything from crying, to masturbating, including reports of a fetus trying to fight off a needle after repeated in-utero medical treatments.

An infant's cry can illicit responses from each member of a social species group, whether the animal is related to it or not. To ignore a baby's cry takes immense self-control.

For the baby, crying comes naturally, and the rewards of its mother's responses begins a life-long process that refines the social talent given many names in many languages: savoir faire, stage-presence, magnetism, influential, convincing. Nice ways of saying 'manipulative'!

It's the intent, of the manipulation, that dictates the positive or negative air about it. When we set out to manipulate the way our animals perceive us, we can do away with social constraints and fire away! Feel free to connive, plan, scheme, and cheat your way to helping your animal understand what it is you want of them.

Manipulation can be fun! If a dog is scared of loud noises we could devise a game where we react the opposite way the dog does to a loud noise...
"BAM!"
"Darn it anyway, that steel bowl just happened to drop on the floor. Here pooch have a little snack."
"BAM!" Oops it happened again!
"C'mon lets lay on the floor and have another snack."
"BAM!"
"What's with that silly bowl anyway? Snack?"
Yawn!
"Tired after all your snacks pup? Yeah, me too"

"BAM!"
"Here, I'll scratch your belly while you nod off."

Most training philosophies require physically negative training with positive re-enforcement, which leaves lasting 'negative' associations with the word, sounds, or cues, that are involved with the command. Through effective manipulation, we can create an environment or scenarios that result in the animal thinking that what it wants to do - just happens to be what we're asking it to do.

The contrast is stark, if we put the "*shoe on the other foot*", and consider which way we would rather be manipulated into 'sitting': 1) pulled on the neck and pushed down... Or 2) Guided, through fluid signals that make us chose to sit, to make it easier to follow the "cue", such as when we hold food above a dog's head. Their skeletal structure is such that, to look up at the treat, it's easier for them to drop their bums to the floor. If we think through our options, when teaching postures or behaviours to our animals, we can find ways to persuade them to learn through 'positive' methods, and avoid negative associations or limiting-behaviours, as a consequence of force-cued commands.

An old dog came into the shelter after its owner died. He was a fat, happy old dog with good manners. He had one quirk. You could ask him to "Sit" with words, hand signals, food held over his head - nothing worked. But, touch him lightly with one finger above his tail and Ploop! Down he'd go! You could pretend to reach out to touch him and he'd just stand there waiting to 'feel' the cue.

* * *

The old dog had been trained in the old push-pull 'standard', and then conditioned to wait for the touch before 'sitting.' This may seem trivial, but the significance is in the old guy denying his own comfort, standing and craning his head up to look at food, not 'thinking' to sit because he hadn't felt the cue. It's likely we were giving him a 'cue' that he knew to mean, he should "Stand". Even in his advanced age he relearned different cues for his old commands. Teaching him that he didn't need to be touched to 'hear' the Sit command was the first and toughest one for him. After that, he was like a snowball rolling downhill, picking up new cues as fast as a young dog.

Being able to manipulate the knowledge or perspectives in a dog's mind, is more powerful than a pronged-collar. It takes work and refining talents on our part.

In order to effectively manipulate an animal we need to be conscious of what motivates them. A horse won't follow you far for a piece of chicken but, they'll crowd you to the ends of the earth for a little mouthful of grain.

Our animals innate needs provide us with a list of "cheats" we can use as motivators. Like the old Carrot and stick routine.

At the top of our dog's list of needs is social contact. The need for socialization is inborn in our domestic animals. It can be exploited as an effective tool for focusing attention, motivating behaviours, and changing perspectives.

The degree of 'neediness' in a dog can be a strong lever when training. The petting game described in the story of Simba, the slobbering bull-mastiff, depicts how our presence and distancing of ourselves from the dog can have profound effects.

The practise of isolating a social species animal during training is age old and has its benefits, especially with fractious or fearful animals. The solitary environment should as much as possible provide a safe 'feel' - broken only by the intermittent attention of the trainer. This helps the animal focus on the individual as the sole provider of all things good. It magnifies the need for social interaction and endears the trainer to the dog.

Keeping a social species animal in isolation for extended periods is not humane, and should only be utilized with adult animals, as an interim step during training or behavioural modification.

The most common, innate need all mammals share is that of sustenance. Food! That wonderful, controllable substance precious to all, and to predictable degrees: not hungry, hungry, really friggin' HUNGRY!

Food is the way to any animal's heart. With proper handling it's also a great tool for demonstrating that we own a VERY important thing. Across the field of animal care experts, new pet owners are encourage to make sure their dog 'allows' them to play with their food while the dog is eating.

This <u>idea</u> is passed along by vets and obedience trainers with good intentions, but can lead to catastrophe for some inexperienced owners and their dogs. The advice they receive often fails to include which tone should be used, or the appropriate response the dog should give to the human who is claiming the food. What this generic advice is intended to do, is to make the dog safe around humans, especially children, while the dog is eating.

On top of that, this 'practise' should be used to clearly communicate to the dog that, the human owns the food. The goal is for us to be able to relay, with a minimum of vocalization, posturing, or drama: "Enough! I want my food back". In return, the appropriate response from the dog would be to move away and relinquish the food, with a submissive toned <u>reply</u> (moving away with ears and tail low, indirect eye contact, or focus on the food).

Now stop! Before you try those talents you've honed in the mirror, beware that ANYTIME you mess with the food of a social animal, you better be prepared for an argument. Bad, bad things can happen!

That religion based edict, to "share and share alike" is not practised by most of the human race, let alone other species - particularly not in times of scarcity! Protect your animal and yourself, from failure and be safe. If you have any suspicion or doubt at all, that your dog may disagree with you claiming ownership of those last morsels of sustenance, don't attempt to <u>own</u> it. First establish your authority and ownership over other, less precious articles -

like a stick or tennis ball. In most cases there won't be a problem, but safety should always be first. Expect the best, but prepare for the worst.

When 'claiming' an object, the best way to "see" it done is to watch well acquainted dogs/wolves feeding. If one comes too close to the Momma's prime pickin's, she'll start communicating with her eyes that she wants the other one to 'back away'. All movement will stop and she'll fix her gaze, hard and strong, on the pup coming too close. If it proceeds toward her, she'll maintain her gaze, perhaps upping the tone of it, and show her teeth in a snarl. If that doesn't work she'll add a low growl to the mix, again changing the tone. If the pup doesn't get it by this time, it's likely the mom will <u>explode</u> toward the pup, with a snap of her teeth. Her intention is not to bite, but to make the pup believe that she is going to, causing him to retreat. When the pup shows visible signs that it understands and is sorry, she removes the 'pressure' and returns to eating, without further hostile body language or expression, letting the pup know that all is well again through her disinterest in him. She'll remain that way, providing the pup doesn't repeat the offence.

The above scenario includes the mother dog using two 'psychological' reins on her pup. Those two reins are our keys to controlling our dogs, and the basis from which a full and natural relationship can be developed. Like the reins on a horse, they can be used to turn a dog, though not in the typical right and left fashion. Instead, they can be used to promote or inhibit any behaviour or action the dog undertakes. Something the dog is doing can become "positive" and encouraged or it can be made "neutral or negative" and discontinued with minimal 'discussion."

These imaginary reins are called "Good" and "No". The word 'sounds' themselves, at first, mean very little to our animals. Though by association with English speaking humans, most dogs, from early on, fairly safely assume the sound "Good" means a treat is coming and "No" means uh-oh, I screwed up again, or I'm in trouble for something.

To help our dogs differentiate between the two reins, we first have to understand their operation.

Let's start with "Good." Few people have difficulty letting their dogs know they're pleased with them or their actions. The number of ways which we can convey "Good" to our dogs is varied.

To our dogs, "Good" should be the word sound it associates with a game pairing its behaviours or actions with cues from the trainer to receive a reward.

In day to day living we also need subtle ways to indicate our pleasure for actions our dogs do naturally as part of living together as companions. Things like, the dog moving off of the human's chair without having to be spoken too; should be able to be accomplished by the owner 'looking' at the dog with and expectant expression. The dog moves and is 'told' good with a smile and a release of pressure from the 'look.'

Alternate ways of saying "good" can include:

- A well timed Treat
- Verbal praise (rhythmic speech, toned to convey excitement and nonthreatening emotions)
- Facial expressions (expressing pleasure, ease of countenance and confidence)
- Body language (conveying relaxed or excited, non-threatening expressions)
- Release of pressure (real or implied), as in eye contact or confrontational stance or expressions - though not released to a posture that might be construed as uncertain or submissive.

With a dog of any age, teaching it the meaning of "Good" is the Foundation Stone to any future discussions or relationship building experiences you will share. In the same way a wild horse can be moved from mortally terrified to comfortable and accepting of a human being in an hour's time, so too can our dogs make huge leaps in understanding. "Good" builds the bridge that all other dialogue flows over.

"No" is the second rein we need our animals to understand. However, proper progressions being what they are we'll finish adding the "Good" Rein first.

Finding "Good"

You know what it means. Your dog knows what it means - just in a different dialect. His mom and litter-mates taught him, long before you came into the picture. We just need to bridge the gap by translating for them.

The best way to do that is to "teach" them something easy.

To start with, clear the environment of any and all possible distractions: other dogs, TV, Facebook chats. Get yourself a tea or coffee, and for the dog, about twenty small pieces of soft, swallow-able treats (frankfurters). Put the dog on a six ft. rope and sit yourselves down for a little "chat."

What we are going to chat about is, what is the dog expected to do when it hears the sound of its name. Easy right?

Our goal is to have the dog understand that, contrary to popular belief, their name isn't a phonetic replication of the name-tag sewn to his raincoat. To our dogs, their name's doesn't herald to the world "George is my name"...

To our dogs, their name should be a "command" that means: "Look at my eyes (briefly)" or "If you can't See me - don't move - Listen! I'm about to tell you to do something important."

More dogs than not, assume their name is a less forceful way of being told to 'come'. Their name should only mean "look" or "listen," not "come running" as in those unfortunate wanderers whose owners only notice their dog's trip across the highway at the same time the semi-truck comes round the bend. An unconscious calling of the dog's name, if improperly taught and misconstrued by the dog to mean "come," could cause considerable regret, pain, and suffering.

* * *

So let's build the bridge for "Good," while teaching the dog her "Name".

If the dog is pushy and keeps trying to get the treats you have on the corner of the table, reset, and have it so the dog is tied, within arm's reach, but unable to push you around. Once set, assume a neutral tone with both body and expression. Ignore the dog. Sneak a treat into the hand you normally feed with.

Rotate your body, or at least upper body, to face the dog. Hold the hand with the treat between thumb and forefinger, in a direct line between your dog's eyes and your own. To start with the dog should not be looking at your face or hand before you call her. We'd like her a little distracted - but only mildly. Indifferent would be good.

Use impeccable timing: when the dog's name is called, the hand in front of the eyes should move slightly, to draw the dog's focus to the area you want him associating with his name. You should be prepared and watching closely. The instant the dog's eyes make contact with your eyes, your treat-hand should start moving to the dog's mouth. At the same time, your mouth releases and drags out a low toned "Goo-oo-ood". Your facial expression, especially eyes, should be fixed but not overly animated. The object is to encourage the dog to fix your eyes with light, transient, eye contact, moving between the treat that is approaching his mouth, and back again to your eyes, that should still be in line with the dog's and the treat. The delivery of the treat should require the dog to do nothing, other than look at you and open its mouth, in time for you to put the food in. Drag out the sound of good until the food touches the dogs tongue. Perfect timing for this would be to stop "good" at the same time the dog swallows - hence the reason for using soft treats.

Reload.

After the first round, the dog will usually be bouncing his eyes between your face, hand, and the place on the table where the treats live. It can be handy at this point, to have a bunch of distractions planned out. Scuffing your foot will work a time or two, knocking a book off the far side of the table might help, having someone drop a metal lid, or have them open the fridge: whatever it takes to have the dog focus its attention somewhere other than those three aforementioned targets. Each momentary distraction allows you the opportunity to repeat the dog's name, and direct it to your eye-line and the treat. Do this, four or five times, then stop for ten or twenty minutes, while you drink your tea or talk on the phone. If you 'absent' yourself from the dog's availability, he'll move on to other thoughts, or lie down and go to sleep. Begin again 'when' you decide it's time to play.

The object is to repeat this process as many times as is possible, without altering the routine, until the dog demonstrates understanding. As the dog looks to your eyes more, the hand can be held into the body, at chest level, for the call. We might have to replace the hand/treat positioning that has helped the dog's target our eyes. We can do that with a quick chin-wag or head nod toward the dog. Eventually and slowly reduce the number and tone of physical cues, until the desired response is achieved with just the vocalization. To follow old Pavlov's recommendations, this exercise should be repeated several times a day for six weeks. After which, the trained behaviour can be defined as being a conditioned response, the be-all-end-all level of training goals.

Classical Conditioning is defined as:

"... as in Pavlov's classic experiments.[2] Pavlov presented dogs with a ringing bell (CS) followed by food (US). The food (US) elicited salivation (UR), and after repeated bell-food pairings the bell also caused the dogs to salivate (CR) (source: wikipedia, classical conditioning)."

It will be essential to delve into this subject deeper in a bit, but for this first "Task" our simple goal should be that at the end of six weeks, repeating the dog's name should cause a down-pour of saliva! Especially from the big mastiff drooling breeds. Another side effect of this conditioning should be the almost painful speed with which our dogs turn to us, if they hear their names behind them. Self-inflicted whiplash!

"Six weeks for THAT?" You say, "A dog I can tie to the door and make drool on command!"

What! Not the kind of parlour trick you had in mind?

Don't worry, it's not a trick just an affirmation that you've built the bridge and can now cross the gap. Don't worry, while you were doing six weeks of THAT! You'll have been busy on a whole bunch of other things concurrently, which will all be ripe for harvest near the same time.

With "Good," your dog has its first Rein on!

It's the most important rein to have on, and well fitted. Properly installed it will ensure a highly motivated work ethic in the laziest of dogs.

It can also be the most difficult to install without errors in timing, judgement, and consistency. Plus, this thing about having to use treats all the time is likely getting old, really fast.

Patience. No rush. If we divide six weeks training over the course of a 12 year life span, it's just a pittance - .009% of the total time you'll spend living with your dog.

A tiny little bit of "Good" goes a long, long way.

"No" means "No"... right?

If we see "Good" as the great motivator and pacifier of the dog world, then "No" is the great inhibitor and clarifier. When "No" is heard, the dog shouldn't scamper from the room, tail tucked, ears back, hoping to miss the swing of the broom. It should just mean "Stop what you're doing."

The tones and uses of "No" are wider ranging in

meaning and effects, than "Good", from the slightest verbal or nonverbal negative translated by the dog as meaning, "No thank you" all the way to a "No" meant to stop a social taboo from occurring. This latter kind of "No", in dog language would mean - in the kindest way a mother can say, "Stop! Or you're toast!!"

Observing the effects of a social species mother saying, "No" can be awe inspiring. To see a group of infants rolling in play or feeding with gusto, suddenly cease all activity with the issuance of a single bark, cluck, or movement, is amazing. The "No" can elicit responses, from stopping an action to calling them back from a dangerous situation.

We can lay a foundation that promotes the same kind of responses from our animals, regardless of environment or stimulus, age or species. Like the process of conditioning the response for "Good," it takes hundreds of repetitions, over at least six weeks, but unlike structured and planned training sessions to develop "Good," "No" can be worked on without treats, through the many opportunities that arise over the course of daily life.

"No" is an awesome word, difficult to teach and implement, but absolutely necessary. Unlike a welcomed "Good," expressed from any one of our language skills, "No," in its various expressions and tones, is rarely a direct <u>comfort</u> passing between us and our dogs. The benefits of well timed, consistent usage of "Good and No" are best appreciated once fully formed, after long-term use.

* * *

Old Benny wasn't born old. His younger years were filled with much frustration and discontent (mostly on my part - he was a little creep!). But with time and patience, *we* grew up, matured, and developed an amazing relationship, with clear lines of communication that, eventually, made him a shining example of communication-based control.

Benny loved to 'work' the clinics that I taught. A lab-rottie has a bottomless pit where others' have stomachs. Clinics always had piles of goodies, and Benny was a pro at getting guests to slide him a few baked goods under the table.

Benny was introduced to the group, after we had played the 'Trainer's Game,' for the first time. Everyone would take a turn being 'clicked' through simple jobs like: picking up a coffee pot and putting it on a table, and then sitting in a different chair. Each person suffered varying degrees of frustration during their turns, which is part of the intended purpose of the exercise. Without experiencing the frustration an animal can go through when we use ineffective communication, it's impossible to wholly empathize with their condition.

The group would be asked to formulate a 'job' for Benny. The task would be similar to what they had just experienced themselves. He'd be asked to pick up a can of pop from the table, or a toy from the counter, and then deliver it to a person or to a specific place. The difference between what they had experienced, and how Benny was worked, was that I used words and hand cues to 'steer' him from one step to the next.

The fluidity of Ben's performance garnered appreciation for his ability to perform unrehearsed and novel tasks by, what the students now understood, was a relatively simple means of communication: especially following so close on the heels of their own moment, with their feet in the dog's shoes. Benny and I had achieved a good set of basic cues that allowed him to be directed through our environment, and to interact in a few simple ways with objects within it. "Good" and "No" were his reins.

Auditory "No's" are essential. A nonphysical cue that does not depend on visual contact can save lives. To say, "No" in a way that dogs can automatically understand, we can make a broad range of sounds, from a sharp intake of breath, to an "Ahh" or a growled "Nooo"! But, as with all things involved with the training of animals, following the proper progression will save time, confusion, and liability.

When a pup first begins to understand "No," it's as part of daily life. Momma will stop them from feeding or pulling on her ear with their sharp teeth, by saying "No" in the form of a mild discipline. Over time, they learn their boundaries, and her cues, that tell them "No" without physical contact. Physical corrections become fewer as their language skills develop - seem familiar?

First, let's review the ways that a mother can say, "No." Canine disciplinary patterns follow stepped elevations of emotionally charged "No's" - starting as small or light in tone as is necessary. This first level is followed by explosive increases in tone and expression, until the desired response is given by the receiver of the signal. Depending on the speed or severity of the <u>misdeed</u>, some of the steps may be skipped, and the mother may go from an <u>eye</u> contact warning to saying, "No" in an extreme way, in the blink of an eye.

She does what she has to!

The normal pattern of escalating "No's" follows this path:

Eye contact - usually accompanied with an abrupt turn of the head or body, to square off toward the target. The gaze is direct and can range in intensity (tone). Eyes rounded, chin lowered, ears turned back, though not flat, muscle tension increased, and gait, if moving, stiffens. If this fails to stop the pup, she goes to the next step.

Snarl or growl - depending if the target is looking in the mother's direction, she will either add a snarl or a growl to the eye she is using, or both. The tone of the snarl or growl will depend on the degree of emotion she wishes to express. With dogs, it's unlikely there is considered 'thought' that goes into the degree of their tones and expressions. Their inhibitions are fewer than ours and, in the case of a mother her tones reflect her 'true' feelings on a subject. As human surrogates we'll need to 'act' sometimes.

* * *

Next is the Snap!

Should the little delinquent ignore the first two levels of "No," the mother adds to her "Eye" and "Snarl" an explosive lunge toward the target, snapping her teeth audibly, aimed at the side of the rebel's head (eye, cheek, neck, or ear area). Her intent now is to force the target to stop its forward movement and flee, or else *risk* being bitten. The mother will use one, or multiple snaps, to ensure instant compliance, though rarely do they make contact or grip at this point.

Examples of these levels of "No" are easy to see, anywhere young dogs interact with old ones. The pups, running and teasing each other around an old guy, are often cut short, when the old dog has had enough and he lets out a series of quick "snap, snap, snaps". The old party poop-ers! A.K.A. Fun Cops!

Last is the Grab - It's rare for a mother to ever need to reach this level of saying, "No". In Dog language, this is the equivalent of being strapped to the electric chair, just moments from death. Even when necessary, the "Grab" rarely lasts longer than a second or two, and contains all the intensity of rage and threatening tones that the mother can muster. The "grab" culminates the preceding actions, with her gripping the pup's throat or neck and possibly giving a slight shake. As a result, the pup assumes a submissive posture - emitting high pitched yelps and rolling onto its back, tail tucked, legs flaccid, and eyes fully dilated. Occasionally, the pup will submissively pee.

* * *

It's from this series of behaviours and responses that modern trainers have mistakenly justified the use of what's commonly termed the "Alpha roll." Rarely, is this degree of "No" justified in the canine world, and certainly never for more than a second or two as we see in the interactions of a mother and her pups.

Dog fights where one dog will latch on and hold another down for an extended period of time are not clear depictions of 'normal' social species behaviour and the use of such exaggerated force on our part should avoided like the plague.

Dog Momma's don't mess around. From an early age, a good bitch will rule over her pups with an 'iron-paw,' for a short time, confident in her decisions and the messages she sends to them. During this time she instills her own version of the "Good and No" reins. After which, they are free to make as many silly mistakes as are safe, and that doesn't bother her or the other pack members. She'll watch them, but can control them quite effectively from a distance; stopping overly rough play or wanderers that are venturing too far from safety.

For us to use the Mother's way of communicating "No" in a safe, humane and effective way, we have to be aware of the consequences of our actions, the potential harm to ourselves and our animals, as well as the possible psychological damage from improper use.

A dog can become discouraged or enraged when it's told "No." Like a child baulking or having a temper tantrum (except with sharper teeth). Untimely or inappropriate "No's" can destroy motivation, confidence, and trust. As with human relationships, trust is a delicate thing and, once broken, difficult and time consuming to mend.

When teaching the meaning of "good" for the first time, we undertook to bridge the gap using the dog's name. When teaching "No," the best exercise is that of claiming and controlling food or articles. Again, **not** for dogs who have demonstrated possessiveness over resources to the degree of being a potential physical threat to humans. Be safe. There are ways around it with those kinds of dogs.

Wars don't start because the sides are in agreement. In that light, rather than jumping right in with a bloody steak and a mortal challenge to see who's the bigger dog, let's start on a less precarious 'battle front'.

The Battle itself is against the misconceptions and skewed perspectives of entitlement, that develop throughout the dog's life when we make errors during the course of daily life with them. Mistakes like being overly permissive, rewarding 'demanding' behaviours, or ignoring tests pups are compelled to try out as part of their normal development.

We can halt those misconceptions and perceptions of entitlement by _owning_ everything, and by being able to start and stop everything that our dogs might do. We get there by being able to say, "Good" and "No" to things they do naturally. As well as being able to cue those things we manipulate them into doing as part of our training procedures.

To wet our feet at saying, "No" in our dog's language, we can use the reliable "greeting" behaviour dogs have. Canine customs dictate that, when adult members return home from the hunt, they be greeted by the hungry pups with nuzzles, licks, and nibbles to the corner of the adults' mouths. With this 'rule of dogs' in mind, it's easy to manipulate a scenario that will make the dog want to lick our faces.

If we come home after a short absence, and lower ourselves to the floor so that our face is within reach of our dog, it will naturally want to do the lick and nibble around the corner of our mouth routine. Even if it's an adult dog that's been taught not to lick a person's face, it will '*want*' to do it.

While moving to the floor, give the dog a fake target to focus on or to smell, our hands work well for this. When we're crouched on the floor, we can lower our head, looking down at the floor in front of us. The dog will poke its nose up into our face, eventually. Dropping our head is the invitation (in dog language). If you don't mind a tongue based face washing, let the tongue-lashing go on for a few seconds.

Then, when we decide it's over, all at once: lift our head, bare our teeth, in a snarl, make our eyes larger, turn our head away from the dog, but only far enough so we can watch its reaction from the corner of our eye, and at the same time, take in a sharp breath (think small explosion). With practise you can make a kind of quiet reverse growl sound. All of these components of "No" need to happen within about a half second. Done properly, the dog should instantly stop licking and step back, changing its focus from our face to "anywhere else." That's their way of saying, "Gotcha! No more lickin'!"

The instant the dog responds as desired, i.e.: first, stops licking, then gives us a little space - all parts of our "No" should stop. Our body and facial expression should return to Neutral: changing from "No," into a subtle, non-verbal "Good" by the release of 'pressure' that the dog felt from our big eyes, tense posture, and sharp intake of breath. To further 'reward' the dog by saying, "Good" is unnecessary. Breaking the silence at this point only stands the chance of distracting or confusing the dog. They need a second or two to let stuff sink in.

After the dog has paused for a beat or two, we can then continue with our own version of greeting them, in whatever way we chose. This exercise is an easy one to set up and replicate. It allows us to start with the lightest of "No's," and amp up the 'emotional' scale to the degree necessary for the dog to understand what "Stop licking my face!" looks and sounds like when you say it in his language.

Again, practise in a mirror to perfect the 'whole' routine before showing off to the dog. Be cautious of your tone.

Face it. If someone you've known all your life welcomes

you in for a lil' kiss, then all of a sudden turns into a wide eyed Cujo telling you to "Stop the contact!" Some of us might strike out in fear! Start with a **light** tone.

Note of contradiction: A 'Momma' has no fear or worry that a pup will 'argue' with her. When she says, "No," she uses the degree or tone that she knows will stop the undesirable behaviour her first try. We want to achieve this same level of authority, and the ability to safely use our full range of "No's." But we have to earn their trust and respect first, to ensure everyone's success and safety.

None of us want to be growled at by anyone, especially our loved ones or bosses, but that's our world, not our dogs. A wee growl, snarl, or snap, from us to our dogs carries a bit of reverse psychology with it that helps clarify, to them, our role as the Mom, and promotes security and calmness within them.

Their tiny little ego's take heed from the "No's" we use, and it comes back to remind them in times of trouble that, "*If Mom can stop me. She can stop that scary thing coming our way!!*"

Having our dog's think about us in this 'idolized' way, allows them to have confidence in our abilities that inclines them to follow and feel secure in as natural a way as is possible. Our consistent, well-balanced "No's" assure them that they don't need to make *decisions* when Mom is around. Our "Good's" and "No's" help our dogs avoid making "Tea-party" assumptions from the plethora of instinctual responses they have to choose from.

191

In our politically correct world, terminology reigns supreme. Thankfully dogs aren't interested in politics. After witnessing how 'knee-jerked' their reactions are to our speaking their language, most people appreciate the benefits of learning to speak our dog's language as a first step in improving relationships and starting training.

To prepare for the next degree of "No" with eyes open and heads clear, I'll reiterate: most dog's will react as they should when told "No," without aggressive outbursts. BUT! There are some dogs who take exception to being deprived of, what they consider an entitlement, and they will pitch a fit! Not the crying, rolling on the floor, or stamping feet of a child, but the canine equivalent, which could include snarling, growling, gnashing teeth, or bites.

Our tone can change the meaning of a "No" from a directional tool, to a soul-cutting curse. We must use our 'powers' wisely and humanely. Where our animals really come from, everything about them is perfect: their language, their behaviour, their drives, and their desires.

When we bring them into our modern world and start to inhibit their natural behaviours, we bear full responsibility for any corrections we have to make. Our failure to teach and communicate with them effectively, does not justify their having to suffer an inappropriate correction, as an excuse for an educational tool.

A bitter truth expressed by Therrien, was never more true: "*If you have to make a correction it's because you're screwing up, not the animal."*

At first it seems an easy statement to argue with, but the more you think on it, the truer it becomes. With the exception of young animals still under maternal care, the rarity of 'corrections' made within social species animal groups that result in physical contact, are few and far between. Our permanently adolescent-minded domestic dogs mature at a stage where their wild peers have long stopped needing the proverbial "cuff up-side the head." Getting 'physical' when correcting our dogs, should be our last option! This is especially true in cases of behavioural rehabilitation, where the dog has likely experienced a multitude of confusing signals. Confusion can build false perspectives, anxiety, and aggression.

We all make mistakes, lots and lots of them. Our dogs might learn from them, or not. Either way, their minds remain plastic, so in spite of ourselves, we can ask more of them than their wild counterparts. We can repair damaged perspectives and renew trust and confidence. It just takes time, patience, understanding and work.

With clients whose dogs are in need of major behavioural adjustments, I encourage patience, and ask them to plan for a third of the time that it took to create the behaviour before they can expect 'it' to be gone. Sure, there are short-cuts, and more times than not problems resolve quickly, but setting them up for realistic expectations promotes patience, and minimizes the chances of people getting 'in a rush' or 'hurting something'.

A good next step in convincing our dogs that we're on their level, is to start using their versions of "No" as part of our communications while playing. In order to start and stop everything, including play, we can use "No" as a simple alternative for "Stop."

At this stage, we want to select a toy or bone that the dog enjoys playing with. We'll start a wrestling match involving the toy. Keep the enthusiasm level in the dog at low to middling. During play, with the dog a short distance away from us, we can drop the toy and look away, as if suddenly interested in something that we just heard rustling behind the curtains.

Play is over, Mom's gone on to new business.

When the dog makes a go for the toy to try and renew the game, stop him with a sharp intake of breath and the evil eye. Include a facial snarl if it's necessary.

Then, when he stops his forward motion and pauses in his attempts to resume play, we can turn our focus back to where it was before (a small silent 'good'). It's just the 'moment' that we are looking for, not a complete, full-stop of the play session, but a brief four or five second pause while you pay attention to something else, then when we're ready, we can resume the play session.

One more successful "No" lesson under our belts!

With practise, our dogs quickly become familiar and

comfortable with the new dialogue we've created. Our rhythm and timing improves, while we start and stop play of higher and higher excitement levels. Learning 'life skills' through play is a familiar theme shared by most young animals. Even as mature adults, we can play our way into becoming fluent in countless new tasks and challenges.

Once we can stop our dog from licking our face and can stop light play in an 'instant,' we're getting on safer ground for bringing out the bloody steak. Following our own instincts and intuition, we can be attuned to when the time is right for the Final Showdown .

The "Raw T-Bone or Bust Challenge"

Prepare for the 'trial' by assembling a plate of irresistible meats and goodies that our dogs won't be able to resist. Prepare your mind, visualizing the actions and explosiveness levels we might have to use. Think about what kind of 'tone' may need to be injected for us to succeed. Much of this will depend on the nature and predisposition of our dog. Like a cross-species form of Tai Chi, we'll want to turn the dog's energy back on itself. Meaning, if our dog is high energy and pushy, we'll need to use an adequate degree of tone and energy to turn him from his goal. If our dog is slow moving, gentle, and not too pushy, we'll succeed with less vehemence in tone and less emotional display.

We'll start by bringing our Plate-o'-Bait to the table.

Our presence should be neutral and calm. Hand feed

the dog a morsel. Then, toss the next morsel far enough away to give us the time to put the plate on the floor, a foot or so in front of us, while the dog makes his way to the food you've just thrown.

We'll turn our body position a quarter turn away from the food. Then, watch with peripheral vision as the dog returns. As it approaches the plate, we'll increase our muscle tension and prepare to rotate back toward the plate. Depending on how fast the dog is moving, we'll have to decide <u>when</u> the appropriate moment is to 'explode' with a "No."

The dog must **not** succeed in getting even the tiniest scrap of food. But he must be close enough to it to understand that it was his position relative to <u>our</u> food, that caused the explosion of "No." This is where we're forced to gamble a little bit. Timing is like that! Getting it right takes practise, and there's no *recreational* way to practise this sort of thing.

During the explosion, we will have used all the components of dog language at our disposal: a low toned, guttural roar of a growl "BAarrgh!" not too loud, but sharp and surprising. A strong intense eye, tense facial muscles, and a fast turn in our seat, to land in a looming posture over the plate of food at our feet with our hands made into snarling claws guarding the plate.

If the dog advances, through this part of the "*I Own This*" speech, we've screwed up and weren't convincing enough in the opening remarks. Shoot your hand out toward the dog's cheek, fingers claw-like to imitate the snapping, snarling, teeth, of its Momma. Set your feet, audibly - growl with intensity and an elevated tone, until the dog says, "Oh sorry, I didn't realize that's your food!" - or something to that effect.

We only want to do this once. It's essential that we do it right. We can practise on a friend first, if we have any worries or doubts about your own ability to effectively relay the message.

Most human males don't have a problem switching on and off, the "Rage Face". Little boys practise it in the mirror, around the same time little girls start wanting to cut the hair off their dolls and use their Mom's make-up. Little boys play at, and develop instinct driven skills evolved from hunting and protecting. Little girls develop instinctually driven skills rooted in nurturing and group function (including many of the hunting and protection roles of the males). Many adult women need to be encouraged to openly demonstrating assertive or aggressive facial expressions or body language. Societal conditioning doesn't help much, with Disney themes or rhymes like "...Sugar and spice and everything nice...".

The forms and uses of "No" must be wielded with humane reserve. Overuse can diminish the dog's confidence and willingness to try new things, or at its worst, break their 'ethereal' spirit and create a dog void of personality and joy. We need to find a balance that allows the dog to explore and learn, both positive and negative experiences, on its own. We can guide them, to avoid injury or damage where and when possible, but over-control can be as damaging as having no limits at all.

Be safe, use visualization and minimize risks, while exploring the timing and rhythm involved in fluently speaking a different species language. Remember, heightened states of emotion make social species animals incapable of 'reasoning'. Start by saying, "No" in situations where emotions are low and our dogs are able to 'think' and inhibit their own responses.

Personal safety must be a primary concern. With dog's that have demonstrated possessive aggression it is recommended that people seek a professional to get them through the rough spots. At the very least, if help is not available, when trying "No" with food for the first time - tie the dog up, so it can only chase you so far if things go awry. Be Careful.

One of the clouded, early memories I carry with me to this day is of wrestling with one of our dogs, as a child. The dog and I were having fun, but it was getting rough. Mom watched us from a distance, and eventually called out in a worried voice: "<u>You're playing too rough! If you get bit, don't come crying to me,</u>"

I wasn't bitten back then, except as a pleasant part of our play. But, the few times since, in my adult life, when I've been tagged by a tooth, that warning comes back to me. Dogs that show up here for aggression problems can be managed safely. If I get 'bit' it is my fault for not covering all the bases and for not being careful enough.

Visualizing all angles, and taking precautions to have fail-safe 'exit' strategies in place, is essential. Having said all that; handling problems of extreme aggression or fear, in adult dogs, is not a good place to start learning from. In these cases, the help of an experienced behaviourist, with a proven track record of humane, positive rehabilitation successes will be the best course of action.

Communication and understanding the animals we're working with is our launch pad to training success. The rest is just mechanics.

CHAPTER FIVE

The Truth about Obedience

By this time in our private sessions, the clients are full to brimming with perspective change and language skills they're dying to try out. Giving them the last few bits of 'Training know-how' is our final section and is usually brief.

Training, as defined by the Merriam-Webster Dictionary, is derived from the root-word <u>Train</u>, used in our context as a transitive verb defined as:

3 a:<u> to form by instruction, discipline, or drill</u>
  b:<u> to teach so as to make fit, qualified, or proficient</u>

That sounds boring, invasive, and not very fun at all. But once more, perspective is what it's all about.

The form of instruction we choose, or how we teach, can make all the difference in the world to how well it's received by the recipient. If we turn our thoughts once again to 'basic' evolutionary schemes, and watch how animals naturally form skills and learn acceptable behaviours, we have to admit that we humans take a pretty mundane approach to <u>schooling</u>.

The argument among scientists over non-human morality, cognition, and language, inevitably touches on the topic of "play": how it relates to social conduct, the animal's intelligence levels, and their abilities to recognize and communicate differences in actions, between real and play among their peers.

What is least contested in these circles, is the value of play to each species, as a developmental vehicle in refining life skills that the animal will need, once maturity is reached. Through play, social species animals learn rudimentary 'codes of ethics' that determine appropriate degrees of: bite pressure, start and stop cues, how to promote or prolong play, as well as, how to communicate which game they want to play. Their games refine survival based skills that relate to: predatory or anti-predatory manoeuvres, cooperative function, or mating behaviours.

If we can form our lessons in a context that our animals perceive as 'Play', the more positive their memory will be of the experience and the longer our training sessions can be. Walking in a circle, with a group of dogs on a leash, following regimented 'Sit - Stay' drills fails to meet this natural form of Learning's "Top ten list" - but, it's a good goal to strive for once the 'play' teaching's been done.

Play can be used at any stage in an animal's life, to

inject enthusiasm into a bored or distracted mind. In our busy, grown-up lives we have a hard time remembering what spontaneous childhood play really felt like. In 'true' play, those parts of our minds that regulate moral codes and inhibitions take a break, while we explore novel compulsions without limiting the experience too much - Freedom of thoughts, expressions, and actions. Whoo Hoo!

Our dogs are not so different.

The learning curve of young animals spikes in their infancy and flattens out as they mature. The amount they play follows a similar path. If we consider the limited mental maturity in our dogs, the advent of domestication created a learning-monster. In a brain that's been forever locked to an adolescent phase, and exemplified in their behaviour, we're free to combine their lifelong joy of playing with never-ending opportunities to learn and do different things.

To effectively use play as a source of inspiration, we need to take the fun out of it for a minute or two.

"Play," in a dog's eyes, is a different movie reel from the one most humans have. Our version of "Play" evolves so quickly, as adults we can just vaguely remember the times before 'structured play' dealt its blow. To find a comparison of play that we can relate appropriately to our dogs, we can think about favoured games of human toddlers: being chased by their parents from one to another, kissing, tickling, and 'love-bitting' sessions, hide and seek, slow motion gentle wrestling, posturing or feigning extreme emotions, or acting crazy and then laughing. Watching a litter of pups going through the course of a day, will provide many examples of the same toddler-type games.

When we consider our 'given needs' as a social species animal, we can see how early play turns us into specialists at developing, not only resource acquisition skills, but also skills related to procuring for our emotional and psychological needs as well. Those *Given needs*, as identified by Griffin and Tyrrell are:

- Security
- Attention
- Sense of autonomy and control
- Being emotionally connected to others
- Feeling part of a wider community
- Friendship and intimacy with someone who is accepting of the total person, flaws included
- Privacy – opportunity to reflect and consolidate experience
- Sense of status within social groupings
- Sense of competence and achievement
- Meaning and purpose

Nine out of ten of the listed 'needs' are easy to imagine human or animal games, oriented to fulfilling one or more of them. Only Privacy needs no bedfellows, yet it still allows for solitary play of its own kind.

* * *

For us to 'play' with our dogs in a genuine fashion, we've got to get on their level. Pulling out the old checker board isn't gonna cut it... Unless! ...We roll the checkers down a flight of stairs and race to catch 'em on the way down.

Spontaneous Play happens, more than it's created. The time and place to dive into a round of Yee-Haw, without it coming off as a contrived set-up, is when distractions are at a minimum and energy levels are highest.

Throwing a stick for a dog is called "Playing Fetch." But compared to a good old fashioned bout of wrestling; that dried up old stick isn't all that cool. Dogs are drawn to play with much the same intensity as addicts are pulled by their vices.

Play between two dogs, grows trust. Mutually agreed too biting is a risky business. The longer and harder they can play together, and maintain the charade of fighting or pursuing, without hurting one another, the closer their relationship becomes. To dogs, the amount of body contact shared in the rolls and tumbles of a play fight, illustrates the degree of trust that's developed between the two. Dogs whose trust levels are high will, if size differences permit, bear the other's full weight while being pinned. They'll exchange gentle play bites, switch roles; grappling each other into submission, all in the name of fun, but with convincing sounds and appearances that in non-play situations, would be terrifying to behold.

Their play can include rolling theme changes; from

play fighting, to running, hiding, stalking, pouncing, capturing and conquering. These can morph into care-giving and mutual grooming, while they rest up. They invite and agree to play with others through body postures, facial expressions, and actions.

The common play-bow of dogs, with their front end dropped low and their hind-ends up in the air, is the classic canine invitation to play. It says to another dog, in a teasing canine tone: "I'm playin'! Are you ready? Huh? Here we go!"

If we can free ourselves to join in their games, our dogs will be as entertained as our toddlers are when we *cut-loose* with them. We're their surrogate mother for life, so it behooves us to play with them as a Mom would, who had a single pup in her litter. She'd fill the role of litter mate to help her pup express and learn through play. When we play with our dogs in 'their way', we provide for some of those innate needs they have.

The importance attributed to having these needs met is a full-time job for an immature dog mind. Their emotional needs are more immediate and consuming, than a parched throat or hungry belly. Consider what makes a dog cry or scratch at the door first: loneliness or hunger. The universal balm for loneliness is social interaction, play.

Dozer, the big white coloured yellow lab who taught me so much in my youth, was a wonderful dog to watch play. From his first 'out of litter' encounter with another dog, at 10 or 12 weeks, he was the epitome of how much dogs love to play, especially with each other.

A group of tourists came to visit from Germany and brought with them a dainty little chihuahua bitch. She was a mature female and he was hardly off the teat, but their antics were the highlight of everyone's trip. Doze' would spend most of his time playing with her from on his back. They'd spar, her jumping in and out of his reach, with gnashing teeth and evil sounding little growls. He'd lay on his side with her posturing over him. She'd stand on his chest with her front feet looking, for all-the-world, like a hairless mini version of David, after he'd slain Goliath.

Dozer would lay there for a moment, defeated, then roll up on his front shoulder and grab her leg in his mouth. Even though he was a pup, his playmate was so small compared to him. Her whole leg seemed to disappear, from her paw to shoulder. He'd hang on to her bird-like leg until she'd flash him a 'look' that intensified her eye contact, the expression would only flash for a fraction of a second, and he'd turn her loose.

At 12 weeks of age, with sharp little baby teeth, he was already attuned to the degree of bite pressure he could use with the tiny boned little dog. He was also learning different forms of persuasion that he could use to try and extend the duration of their play sessions.

Teasing was one of the ways he learned first. When she'd had enough of him, he learned that he could sometimes 'push' her into one more round, by running toward her and deke-ing away at the last second. Most times she'd give chase. Dozer's klutzy infant gait didn't give him any hope of getting away. She'd be on him in an instant and away they'd go again: Dozer on his back, the little chihuahua giving him the <u>beating</u> of his life. The two were as unfairly matched as a mouse and an elephant, but in play, anything is possible! The little mouse of a dog, won every time, and she loved him for it.

To play with them in their way, we have to get off our feet and down onto the floor. Sharing moments, without intent as part of a rolling dog-pile creates a bond like nothing else. When we first start out playing their way, we'll get scratched and bumped. As we grab each other, they'll get carried away and bite too hard. But, like the little Chihuahua, we can *discuss* all this while we play. Wrestling around with our dogs can be viewed as a dance. They'll learn how to regulate their actions in order for us to keep playing with them. And we'll learn to read their excitement levels and how to rein them in without ruining the mood.

Acceptance of risk and liability should be a foregone conclusion for anyone who calls a dog, 'Mine'. They're a muted version of an animal that hunts, bites, and kills creatures for a living! Chances are, through accident or malign intent, at some point in our life with dogs we're going to get bit. When that happens, the first question we ask shouldn't be "Why did you bite me?" But rather "How did I cause that?"

* * *

People have a tendency to take things too far. For years, the verdict has been in and the signs have been printed. They read "Don't allow your dog to play-bite." This is often inappropriately translated as, "Don't let dogs put their mouths on you."

To inflict this kind of restriction on an animal whose closest appendage to our opposable thumbs is his tongue - is akin to allowing English to be spoken, except limiting its use to words without the letter "E." A Dog's 'bites' can be used for so much more than pain causing. Bites are part of mutual grooming, expressing affection and initiating play. Allowing ourself to be bitten in these ways, displays trust and a measure of reciprocated affection. In this light, "Play" becomes our own teacher. If we start playing slowly and gently, increasing the exuberance and amount of "taboo" actions we allow the dog to experiment with, we will learn to steer the games and emotions. This will ensure we can maintain safe arousal levels, starting and stopping at any time - instantly - yet striving to retain a carefree air about the whole event.

After developing the ability to fall in and out of play, we're free to start injecting learned behaviours, or start forming new ones, during short 'breaks' in the festivities.

Learning is best done in baby steps. An infant human has to learn how to roll-over onto its belly before it learns to crawl. As our talents and muscles develop, we learn to stand, and then walk. We're one of the most helpless infants in the animal kingdom. If we keep our own <u>start</u> in mind, it helps to add patience to our dog training expectations. Waiting for an animal to completely learn the first part of a skill, before adding more difficult ones, takes time. We're often too impatient to use progressions for training, but the benefits can't be denied.

Young dogs can be a handful, but contrary to appearances and the behaviour of some, they don't really spend their days planning ways to piss us off. Their immature mental state propels them to seek constant reassurances that they "belong." They spend a lot of their time guessing and trying, many times failing, to acquire the 'attention' they're programmed to seek.

We've talked about Understanding the canine mind, where they come from and how they think. We've talked about how they communicate and what kind of things blow-their-hair-back. We've discussed natural reins with which to promote or inhibit behaviours. Now let's put it all together in a neat little package and put it to good use.

There are many theories and styles of training. Some are more palatable to our senses, though fail to produce results. Some forms are abhorrent in their physicality and appearance, though produce passable results. Many popular forms of 'obedience' training classes and methodologies are derived from practises made popular decades ago, freshened up with a new coat of marketing paint, and reissued with little change in theory or perspective.

The Kohler brother's from the 1950's popularized what we know today as, "Obedience classes". At the time, they were Film-making golden-boys, providing domestic and wild animals for any number of television and feature film projects. They produced results, and were trusted to come through for their clients.

They taught their clients the use of: lumping-sticks (wooden dowelling covered in rubber hose), prong-collars, choke-chains, and throw chains. Their dog training method focussed on Negative training with Positive reinforcement. For example: A dog is told to heel, a collar correction puts the dog where it should be. If the dog stays in the right spot it is rewarded by not feeling another collar correction. This is repeated over and over again, until the dog understands the word "Heel" means *"Hurry up and get beside the leg before the chain jerks the hell out of its neck."*

For each cue the dog learns in this style of training another life-long negative association is created. Not surprisingly, some dogs can't learn under these pressure laced conditions. Negative training isn't *all* bad - But using it as a first line tool is a poor choice.

Some negative reinforcement practices can compliment positive training styles but, they need to be held in reserve to correct misbehaviour after a command is trained in a positive fashion. Using negative reinforcement in this way Focuses the *correction* on the animal's failure to perform. Lessening the chances of jeopardizing positive associations we've developed surrounding the cue and related behaviour.

* * *

As an alternative to negative training, we can use positive training with positive reinforcement. Positive training depends on nonphysical, passive leading techniques to bridge the gap between our cues and the correct response from the dog, resulting in a reward for successful attempts.

Nonphysical, passive leading can be explained as using the animal's natural desires or needs to create a situation or alter the environment whereby, the animal is faced with minimal choices and only one choice provides for its needs. If we've set it up right, that choice just happens to be what we wanted them to do!

Teaching a pup to sit by holding a treat over it's head is a good example of this method. If we hold a treat up and wait, the pup is faced with three choices.

    1.   Crane its neck, stretching muscles that tire out quickly to keep that sumptuous little morsel in sight. Or,

    2.   Relax his neck and maintain eye contact with the treat by plunking that little bum down on the floor. Or,

    3.   Ease its neck tension by *not* looking at the food (yeah like that's gonna happen!)

Another scenario would be when trying to get a young dog to cross a creek or river for the first time. It's rare to find a dog that can't swim, but most have apprehensions when they're faced with large bodies of water for the first time.

A "Negative" training solution to this would be either picking the dog up and carrying it into the water before releasing it. Or, by pulling it into the water on a leash. Either method physically 'forces' the animal into what it perceives as a fearful new environment. The dog's limbic system will kick in and its survival skills will auto-pilot the animal through the event. Leaving traumatic impressions surrounding water that it may harbour for the rest of its life.

A "Positive" training solution would be to select a calm pool of water in an isolated area and sit in shallow water leaving the pup on shore and wait for it to eventually splash in to see us of its own free will. When hiking we can unceremoniously cross a narrow creek while the pup builds up its courage to wade in. We can wait 'unemotionally' on the far side with our backs to the (sometimes) frantic pups. The more steps we take away from them with the water between us, the greater the pressure is for them to 'make up their minds.' The dog will quickly decide, of its own accord, that being alone on his side of the creek is a worse place to be than facing the scary water that stands between its greatest source of comfort. Once they do it one time of their own volition its not long before they lunge into water without hesitation.

If we observe the teaching strategies of a mother dog, it's based on leading and showing her pups, interspersed with opportunities for them to try, and sometimes fail, without undue pressure or distractions. We can borrow from nature and try to emulate what the Mother does when rearing and teaching her pups:

- limit distractions
- provide easy, then progressively more difficult, tasks as the pup advances in knowledge and ability
- maintain as light and fun environment as is possible, to promote focus and duration of teachable times
- end the lesson before the dog's attention begins to wane

Two popular buzz words with trainers are: repetition and consistency, both of which have their place, though require awareness on the human's part to use properly.

Repetition: instills understanding and confidence, when a lesson is taught in an appropriate fashion. Its use over time can lead to a degree of training that ensures performance and predictable behaviours

Consistency: in what and how we say or do things with our dogs minimizes confusion and speeds learning.

However, consistency also has a potential side-effect which can result in undesired routines being formed. For instance, if we have taught our dog to come, sit, lie down, stand up, and speak, then every time we 'work' the dog, consistently making it: come, sit, lie down, stand, then speak; it won't be long before the dog, when told to "come" - arrives at your feet, sits, lies down, stands up and barks, all without further motivation.

When that occurs we've developed an unwanted 'routine.' To keep our dog's guessing at what we'll do or ask from them next, keeps them on their toes and alert.

Too much routine is boring, no matter what species you are.

Whether Positive or Negative training styles are used, repetition of cues linked with actions that result in a reward, creates understanding. The cues we use are the mechanical parts of training. Timing the reward with the dog's action following our cue is the key.

Use of training Progressions:

Before getting down to the nitty-gritty of actual training, there's a couple more little topics clients are introduced to before getting to the Sit-Stay part of the session.

Training progressions are a planned set of natural steps we can take when teaching our dogs. The right steps at the right time help produce well rounded animals that can be called upon to perform a number of behaviours or jobs throughout their lives. Progression plans are precious for developing working dogs of any discipline, from land or water retrieval, to seeing-eye dogs, or police dogs.

A Training Progression plan is a predefined list of behaviours that the animal will need, when it is called upon to perform its 'job,' once it is trained. With this list, while the animal is still young and malleable, we can encourage some behaviours and moderate others to ensure that the dog's education will progress with fewer hurdles. We can be diligent about not creating negatives that could be associated with future jobs the dog might have.

For an example of using a progression plan we'll write one up for a dog who will be a *Bird-dog*. To build the plan we'll work backwards, starting with making a list of all the things the dog will need to know once it's all grown up. We'll use the Job Description of a Water-dog, as described on Wikipedia:

> "*Retrievers are typically used when waterfowl hunting, although they can also be employed in hunting upland birds as well. Since a majority of waterfowl hunting employs the use of small boats, in winter conditions retrievers are expected to remain sitting calmly and quietly until sent to retrieve. As birds move into range, a well-trained retriever will watch and follow the handler's gun as he shoots, marking, and remembering each bird that is downed. This is called "marking off the gun", and the downed birds are called "marks". Once the shooting has ceased, the handler commands the dog to retrieve each bird that has been downed. If a dog did not see the bird fall, a retriever takes direction from the handler, who can use hand and whistle signals to guide the dog to the unseen downed bird. This is called a "blind" retrieve. During a typical day of shooting, it is not uncommon for additional birds to be downed while the dog is performing a retrieve. Retrievers*

are taught to ignore these "diversions" until the
current retrieve has been completed. Also, at
times, multiple dogs are used on a hunt, and
retrievers are taught to "honour" another dog's
retrieve, by remaining calm and quiet while the
other dog is working."
(http://en.wikipedia.org/wiki/
Gun_dog#Retrievers)

If we analyze the above paragraph, we can make a list of what the dog's job will look like. They'll have to:
- retrieve birds from land and water
- travel in vehicles and small boats
- Be capable of multiple retrieves (marking)
- Blind retrieves
- Directional commands
- Straight A-B-A routes
- ignore distractions
- work quietly, with other dogs in the same vicinity

With this list made, we can breakdown each point and figure out how we can promote these behaviours as the dog grows. At the same time, being careful to avoid putting up stumbling blocks.

If we imagine we're starting with a brand new pup straight from the litter we've got a clean slate to work with. Aside from all the lovin' and cuddling the pup will need, we'll start with the 'basics' that are prerequisites for any progression plan. The first step would be to start the pup learning its name. Followed by orienting it to its new environment. Pups usually need help acclimating to their new social group. We can ease that for them by providing activities that it can relate from its time in the litter; grooming, gentle games of wrestling or pursuing, and my favourite snoozin' together after a big meal.

Regardless of the dog's age, we should put our 'plan' into effect as soon as we get home. Our actions or the lessons we teach, whether on purpose or by accident start being interpreted by the animal immediately.

Say we let the pup go cruising through the house and he wanders into the bathroom and comes out dragging a towel.

If we took the towel from the pup and scolded him for "Dragging things around." We might discourage him from dragging our stuff but, there's a potential side effect. A few weeks later, when we throw his first retrieval dummy the pup might go bounding over to to it then — nothing. He might stand there looking back at us from the dummy with a questioning look. We'd think, "What kind of retriever is this?"

He might be one that learned too quickly that retrieving a towel (or anything else) is a bad thing. When we make an error like this, we have to do a whole bunch of work to *re-teach* something that the little guy did naturally the first day we brought him home. Using a training progressions plan helps minimize this kind of error.

In terms of our Bird-dog plan, we can make sure natural behaviours the dog exhibits early on are not quashed by our own unrelated agendas. If we live on a farm and have chickens we need to keep the pup away from them. If we have to stop the pup from chasing chickens before we take them hunting, we can cause confusion the first time they're asked to bring back a grouse or duck.

From the start we can begin acclimating the pup to all different kinds of environments, animals, people and vehicular travel. If our pups will be asked to work along side of other dogs we can help understand that In-the-field, play is not acceptable, but once out of the field normal socialization if fine.

Knowing a Bird-dog will be in close proximity to gunfire we will have to start early getting them used to the terrifying blast of a fire-arm. A good way to start this kind of noise desensitization is to start the pup's feeding times with a loud bang (drop a pan on the floor, etc...) a second before giving them their supper. If we make loud noises mean a good thing is about to happen our pups will look forward to the gun's discharge when its time to hunt.

Young pups are impressionable little creatures. If we know where we're going, leading is easy and our pups will bound along behind us. Drawing out a clear picture of where we want to go with our young dogs provides us with a crude map.

Every journey begins with a first step. Where we start training our pups is an important part of those first steps.

* * *

When we start training, we should look for a place of quiet isolation. Training any social species animal is best done in a one-on-one environment. Herd-bound animals can only give us part of their attention. Distractions multiply the difficulty and length of time it takes for animals to learn new behaviours.

In a perfect world, this place would be a round room with no doors or windows. Sound-proof. A sterile environment.

As the animal learns in this sterile environment we can add distractions in a controlled fashion: a chair, a coat, the sound of other dogs, the sight of another dog, a dog in the room, etc., increasing the level of interference or distraction as the dog succeeds.

A mother teaches the simplest things first, so our Progression Plans should start with all the most basic 'words' first. Good, No, Name, Come, Sit and down.

Dog's brains are malleable and they have scads of energy. Teaching one thing at a time has been touted as beneficial, but this advise taken literally, can work in the opposite direction. Too much repetition of any one thing can sour a dog's drive to learn. The smarter they are the quicker they learn - and then become bored. Boredom dampens motivation like few things can. It's in that light that I encourage clients to maintain a fun tone, with energy and surprises around every corner, teaching distinctly different commands (one at a time) at different times of the day. Slowly putting different commands together, after they've been accomplished separately. Start training sessions when the dog is least expecting it, and end them on a "Good note", before the dog is ready to stop on its own should be our goal. Own the games and retain the novelty. Training fifty times a day for ten seconds will produce better results than teaching one lesson a day for an hour.

Okay, so! We've made our Training Progression Plan, all those tedious little things we'll have to teach to make a good four-pawed citizen. Here's a sample of a basic plan outline we could use for a family's pet:
- Name/"good"
- Mom owns everything/"no"
- Mom starts and stops everything/"play" and "quit"
- "Come" to mom
- Simple retrieve
- Sit
- Down
- Stay
- Heel
- Stand still
- Come
- Vehicular travel
- Animal distractions

The intention with this list is not to delve into the mechanics of training quite yet, but to round out the understanding of how a "training progression plan" can help us. The mechanics of training are simple. They have to be, in order to make sense to the dog. As a result, the language and application of any training needs to be made up of concise baby steps then, combined with others to create routines that turn into multi-stepped jobs. The first few items on our to-do list are straight forward and only require one step or degree of understanding; a cue or stimulus is linked to a behaviour and a reward.

The simple retrieve starts to add degrees. In order to accomplish the task, the dog needs to: watch the deployment of the target, "go to" the target, pick it up, carry it, then return with it to us, and relinquish the object as the final step. Not so simple after all, or is it?

As long as time and patience aren't contributing factors, the process is simple. There's just more baby steps involved than one would initially think, especially considering that a 'fetch' is one of the most popular dog-human pass-times. With the target of simplicity in focus, we can reduce any of the more complicated routines, like "Get me a pop", down into simple stepped behaviours. Teach each step individually, and then stitch two or more together to form a routine. It just takes a bit of practice and understanding; creativity helps too.

Whether your dog is brand new or well established in your life, their permanently immature mental state allows them to remain malleable throughout their lives.

We can teach old dogs new tricks. Sometimes old dogs are easier to teach than the young ones. A young pup comes straight from the factory, with an over abundance of energy and anxieties, geared toward helping it fit in its new home. Our older dogs may be complacent and require a little motivation to get up off the floor and take on new challenges. Following the "Momma's way," we can reignite our old dog's motivations quite well.

One story of an old dog going back to school happened years ago during one of the weekend clinics we put on. The group was a lively blend of professionals and lay persons who all came together to learn different ways of improving their dog's lives. One participant, an honest to goodness 'rocket scientist' was investigating her options while contemplating getting her first dog. We had talked on the phone and decided that the content of the weekend clinic would give her a more in depth look at pet ownership than what she could find researching on her own, at dog parks or in books. Another participant in this same clinic was a busy obedience trainer who was having problems motivating her own dog, a mature female labrador.

The trainer's dog would perform her standard commands, but did so with little enthusiasm. Her owner complained about being able to motivate the dog to learn or do new things. My guess at the time, was that the Labrador had soured or become bored from repeating old commands without adequate new stimulation to maintain her interest in learning and performing for her owner.

When the topic of training progressions planning was reached I invited the group to come up with a novel "job" we could break-down and make a progressions plan for. Our Scientist offered up the task of training her future dog to start and stop experiments she was working on by going across the room and pushing a button.

It was a perfect task to use so we broke it down into tiny steps and then using the Trainer's dog I showed how quickly the job could be taught.

The Lab had been bored with the classroom proceedings and brightened up when I called her over from her owner and gave her an invigorating ear scratching. She enjoyed the attention and break from the monotony. I worked on her with touch and tone to encourage a playful mood. When she was ready to start playing I grabbed a Dry-erase marker from the table, stopped playing and held the capped end of the writing tool at nose level a short way from the dog's nose. She stopped playing and looked at what I was holding. As she started to move toward it out of curiosity I quietly said, "Touch it." The instant her nose made contact with the Marker I gave her a loud "Good!" While I stretched out the sound of "Good" I put a treat in her mouth. After she'd swallowed the treat I went back to rough-housing with her for a second or two and then repeated the action of holding out the capped marker and asked her to touch it.

Her reward for the first touch had resulted in a double treat; she'd received a treat and then we'd gone right back to playing. The second time she heard "Touch it!" her nose shot out and touched the target like she'd been doing it for years. She was a smart girl and turned, expecting the treat, as soon as she'd completed the task.

Within 10 minutes, in front of a group of people, the Lab could be made to wait while the pen was set up across the room; its capped end hanging over the edge of a table. When told to "Go Touch it," she made her way straight to her target, pushed it with her nose then returned to where I sat waiting to give her a treat and play with her for being such a good girl. The spell was broken and her owner saw how easy her dog was to motivate using the right combination of rewards.

Food leading:

Food is our dog's most precious resource. Its absence is second only to Thirst, for a 'full-bodied' response in times of scarcity. Proper use as a "focus enhancing" motivator, provides a greater range of positive based steering tools than old school forms of motivation that use fear and physical manipulation. A Dog's neurally based drives to "stock up!" are strong, easily controlled and moderated. Using proper food-leading techniques We can control our dogs using no more energy than is needed to fuel our expressions and hand movements while we hold the food used to lead with.

Limiting the amount of the target (food) the dog can see creates visible responses. The best food to use in an example of this is the humble wiener (frankfurter).

The wiener can be beef, chicken, tofu or soy; as long as your dog loves it. Break the top inch off and hold it between the fingers of one hand. In the other hand, hold the rest of the wiener. See the difference between the two?

So do the most "Intellectually Challenged" dogs. Look at the two pieces again. Which one "excites" you most? This is presuming, that you love the same kind of wieners your dog does.

What we are looking for here is the *emotional* response the dog exhibits when it watches the wiener, while we move it around in front of him. Food "*Feels good*" and, by association, everything in that moment is washed in the same light. The more feel-good emotions and thoughts we or our dogs have, the more apt we are to perform, act, react, and move with vigour. The opposite is also true. The more Neutral or Feel-bad emotions the animal is experiencing, the more likely they are to slow down. Being able to subtly control those emotions is like having a dimmer switch on a hyper-active pre-schooler.

With the glorious wiener, we have that dimmer switch. The more your dog sees of it and the closer it is to his mouth, the more excited he's going to get. Palming the wiener and curling our hand in toward our body will cause the dog to exhibit anxious expressions and body language when they lose sight of their objective. Revealing a small portion of the wiener should produce expressions of emotional relief and renewed interest.

To be good at using food as a motivator, it's important to keep in mind the effects we are going to have on the dog's emotions and experience: our timing, the tone of our movements, and expressions, the effects of our eye contact. We call it food-leading, but what we are really doing is teasing the animal with a bit of food.

225

Teasing has it's evolutionary roots in play and as much as we all hated being "Teased" as youngsters there are benefits to the experience. Young social species animals use teasing as an initiator for play from a young age and the lessons stay with them all their lives.

A common scenario to witness in a pair of dogs is when one is tired and no longer wants to play. The younger dog, who still wants to run and be chased will carry a ball or precious stick toward the tired dog, shaking the stick or tossing the ball to emphasis how much fun it's having. As the young dog nears the tired one they will often fumble the ball or drop it completely and then back away. Eyeing the tired dog, as much to say, "Want it? Have it!" They might drop into a play-bow waiting for the other dog to look at the ball, then swoop in and grab it, then run in a small circle trying to tease its playmate into one more go!

Food leading takes practice to use. Each dog responds to teasing in their own way and according to their desire for the article we're teasing them with. Understanding their response to 'teasing' takes a little practice but it's fun!

Try it out with the dog tethered and a little hungry. Observe his reactions to your teasing him. How does he react when you give him a small bite, then back away and show him the whole wiener for a second or two? What happens when we hide it from his sight?

Notice how he responds with the food closer or farther from him. At what point in time or distance does he "give up" and look at something else. How close does the food need to be before he snaps at it? These are cue's we'll take from them, in predicting their behaviour and responses surrounding food drives. The more familiar we are with our dog's inclinations, the better we'll be at predicting what they'll do, and how they'll do it.

Some dogs with strong food-drives can be very 'snappy' when taking treats from our hand. The trick to minimizing pinches and nips from greedy little guzzle-guts is to cool their jets by enfolding the food in our palms and presenting their mouth with our closed hand. Once the dog's mouth has made contact and its tongue has confirmed there is no food available - the dog will keep its teeth away and lick a little more. This allows us the opportunity to rotate our thumb and index finger inline with their mouth. Then, in a controlled fashion, we can let a bit of food escape onto the dog's tongue.

After we've succeeded in hand-feeding without dings and nicks to our fingers we can move on to teaching the dog follow, not just with his eyes, but with his body. Ye olde carrot 'n the stick routine! Start by having her follow our hand with the wiener, as we pivot around in a circle, then to a figure eight pattern, our hand stretched out leading the "Nose" that's flailing to get the rest of the dog closer to treat.

Keeping the right distance between dog and dessert is critical. If the food is too close; the dog's nose can produce a blinding effect. They can become too 'consumed' if the food is on the tip of their tongue the physical task we're leading them through can go by unnoticed. If they think they're on the verge of being 'paid' everything else is peripheral. Each dog has its own 'distance,' when starting out with this. Ideally it should be no closer than one or two feet.

Frequency of payments is important in retaining their attention. Remember the clanging spoons of the trainer's game, the more tiny 'goods' we get, the easier it is to find the way. The more "Payments" your dog receives, the better hold you'll have on his attention.

After we've mastered the basics of food-leading, it's a matter of increasing the amount of distance, and the length of time between rewards, yet still maintain their focus. Keep in mind Pavlov's dog and the repeated bell rings. If, for the first six weeks of using food leading techniques, we never fail to reward the dog, timely and appropriately, the conditioned responses we instil will be all the stronger. This is the start to developing unbelievable working distances and distraction-proof skills. Not only for those folks wanting to create a working dog, but also for developing brilliant pets that, 'fit' into our lives.

Food should be used carefully, and only relied upon as an initial focus-magnet and to help bridge between behaviours and cues. In most cases, the 'hand cue' that goes with a behaviour will be the result of the food-leading process that promoted the behaviour: ie: a finger raised up and pointed over top a dog's head to make it sit, is likely the product of holding food over the pup's head when it first learned to sit. The gestures can be minimized from their "B-I-G," easy to read, beginnings, and made smaller and smaller as part of a game.

Getting away from food leading, as soon as possible, is important. The only 'need' for food in training is as a conditioning tool. Once the six week conditioning period is over, the positive association to the command and action has been conditioned, and food can start to take a back seat.

We can do this after several behaviours have been conditioned. Up to this point they've been receiving "Full-Payments" - a spoken "Good" and a food reward - for each performance.

To get away from "needing" food to make our animals perform we introduce the dog to inconsistencies. We can join two commands in sequence - "Come," "Sit - giving the dog small payments ("Good" only), between "Come" and "Sit". And then rewarding them with a full payment after the dog completes the "Sit."

We can slowly work up to five or ten behaviours in between full payments. Inconsistency here is the key. For the past six weeks our dogs have been paid for every behaviour we ask of them and will have grown to expect a full payment each time. When we start paying at irregular intervals they take up the challenge and accept small payments as if they were a full payment. At this point we want to keep them guessing when they'll get a real mouthful. Ending each short training session with a full payment helps change their expectations. As we add time and cues between full payments each "Good" they hear from us turns into a "Promise of food." With our ultimate goal, to one day have that big bowl of kibble we put down at the end of the day being payment for of all the "Goods" they heard during the day.

When to Train - Our effect on our dog's performance

Relationships are like a dance.

Sometimes, toes get stepped on and people go stumbling.

If we start stepping on our dog's toes when we're trying to teach new things, we're often better off to stop for a moment and consider what we might be doing, or not doing, that could be causing the miss-steps.

Being little sponges, our dogs pick up on our emotional states with surprising skill and with more accuracy than we're sometimes aware of ourselves. Subtle things we sometimes try to hide from acquaintances like moods, internal distractions, anxieties, or fears, can all have effects on what our dogs read into our countenance. If our messages are inappropriate to the situation, the dog will, in some rudimentary way wonder why - and a distraction can be created. If our mental state isn't up to speed, we need to be cognizant enough to know that in that moment, we are getting in a rush and might be better off doing something else.

* * *

We should train when we 'feel' like it, and know our dogs well enough to avoid unnecessary 'difficult times', particularly when we're first starting out. For instance, after a long day of Farmer's Market shopping and a trip to the vet for a check-up: after supper the pup is going to be too pooped to put much heart into trying to get that extra ten feet on a "Stand, Stay" command.

Dogs will never tell on you if you give them a few days off from training. They won't tumble backwards and turn up clueless because we needed to focus our attention elsewhere for a bit. We should train when we're inspired to, not because it is some self imposed edict that says, "At 3:45 p.m. Dog Training time!"

In some ways training is like an art form that suffers when forced.

A good frame of mind to be in is when we can clear our heads of internal distractions or external concerns. If we can enter into that imaginary Round Room, with no doors or windows, and get ourselves "In The Groove" with our animal, sharing time, space, and attention, using language and forethought to manipulate the animal's emotions and behaviours - then we are training, the way we should. When we should be.

The Mechanics of Obedience:

At this point, with all our tools in place, we should be ready to enjoy marked improvements in our relationships and communications with our pets. If we've effectively filled the roll of Mom in our dog's eyes, obedience training becomes elementary.

To most people, Obedience classes are group events where various aged canines, all with immature brains, congregate to learn new skills and frustrate their owners. The topics covered in these classes include skills that are espoused to enhance a dog's chance of becoming a good <u>canine citizen</u>. Classes are usually six weeks long and held once or twice a week. The behaviours covered normally include: Sit, Stay, Come, Down, and Heel, and usually include coaching on how to minimize common behavioural issues like: jumping up on people, leash pulling, barking, and mild cases of aggression.

The Mechanics of Obedience are the physical actions we're going employ to teach the dog the behaviours we want it to perform.

With what we've discussed about food leading, it's mostly just a matter of starting with the food in the right place and going from there. First we'll manipulate the dog's attention, and then body, toward the appropriate responses.

The following 'Mechanics' will outline how to start

teaching the most common Obedience Class commands. We will be in close proximity to the dog as they start learning. As they succeed we'll work toward adding distance between us and length of performance in small incremental steps.

Sit - was earlier explained as being accomplished by holding food above the dog's head, causing it to lower its bum to more easily see its target. With repetition of this process, and well-timed rewards, it's a done deal with even the youngest pups. We can slowly reduce the dogs attention on the food by making the food less visible while maintaining the hand position that will eventually be the visual signal. The actual spoken cue can be added at anytime as an accompanying part of the visual cue.

I encourage clients to delay the auditory cues for commands until the dog is displaying a good understanding of the visual cues.

Down - is the natural thing to teach after our dogs learn to 'Sit.'

For nervous dogs, this position can be their least favourite. Take pains to avoid negative associations surrounding this behaviour. Once more, a sterile environment with no distractions is the best place to start.

The Food leading technique called for in this behaviour is to have the dog sitting, show it the target in our hand, as we lower it to the ground in front of them. The trick here is to find the 'sweet spot' to place the food in. We want to draw the dog's nose after it and down toward the floor.

Dogs are all different. With some, if we put the food under their chin and move it down their chest, they'll slide right into place - others, they will want to get up so they can move back to easily see the food. Good food leading skills help with this part of training. The sweet spot for food positioning for this command calls on us to place the food just the right distance from their nose. Pulling back our hand to touch the ground close enough to make looking down at it uncomfortable to the dog, causing them to slide down onto their chest into the "Down" position.

We can cheat with all kinds of props. With a smaller dog we can turn our bodies sideways to them, sitting on the floor with one leg under us and the other made into an arc. Reaching through the arc, we can food lead them "under the bridge" into a "lay down" when they have to crawl under to catch the food.

For some high energy dogs anchoring them on a tether will help stop them from leaving a sit to 'chase' the food.

A common mistake people make when teaching 'down' is, when they get the dog's attention with food, then as they lower it to the floor and the dog starts going down, the human distracts the dog's thoughts and actions by *saying*, "Down!" The noise of the word often halts the dog's progress, bringing their eyes away from the food and back to the person's face. We can surmise the dog looks up to see the person's facial expression to make sure "Down" isn't a new way of Momma saying, "My FOOD!" Visual cues will always be a dog's first choice for direct communication, learning our language is going to take them some time.

As far as progressions go, we'll sometimes be offered a bonus 'behaviour' while food leading our pets into new behaviours. Often when a dog first lies down, they'll get down on their belly and crawl toward the food if it is held too far in front of them. If they do this, we can make the choice to 'cue' the dog to crawl while it's doing it on its own. I've often modified the hand signal for 'Down' into an imitation of a spider, lopsidedly hauling a chunk of wiener away from the dog, as its 'crawl' command.

Being prepared to capitalize on things our dogs do naturally can add colour to our dogs repertoire. By using our reins of "Good" and "No," we can promote natural manoeuvres our dogs perform of their own free will, and create unique behaviours, that we'd otherwise be hard pressed to develop through other means of teaching.

Come - The easiest way to teach "Come" is with one person holding the dog and releasing it when the trainer cues the dog to 'Come' from a short distance, weenie in view.

One person can accomplish the same thing by baiting the dog away from them by throwing a small piece of food. When the dog finds the bait and turns to look back at us, we can call their name to get their attention, give them a small payment for looking ("good") followed by a cue to "come."

As the dog progresses and distances are achieved, we

can use 'emotion' to make them hurry up. Try running away from them as they come toward us. Our 'leaving' increases their urgency to be near us and usually results in a burst of speed while they try to catch up.

During the course of everyday life we're presented with multiple opportunities to develop this behaviour. Having a bowl of treats handy during our dog's first few days with us, can really accelerate the learning of this cue.

Stay - is best taught in the progression after Sit and Down have been taught; around the same time as we teach 'come' but not in conjunction with it, especially early on.

A dog that is initially released from a 'stay' by touch, will have an easier time progressing to longer 'down-stays', than a dog that is called off a 'stay' too early. They'll come creeping around the corner, as much as to say, "Uhmm... Did, I hear you say 'come'? I could have sworn I did."

As with other new behaviours, we start small and get bigger. Initially making them 'stay' for a beat, then working up to seconds, minutes, then hours! Starting from close range, and working all the way up to extreme distances, with the trainer absent in sight and sound.

The old weenie plays a big role at the start of this one too. A hand held up in the universal sign for "Stop," with our thumb clamping the wiener to our palm, will become the hand signal. With the dog sitting, we'll sweep our hand up, in front of the dog's nose, then pull it back away from them. At first, we can only expect a momentary pause before the dog will start rise and approach. Timing is everything. A slow dog will give us lots of time to get our message across. Whereas, a fast, food driven dog will only sit for a fraction of a second before wanting to chase the hand-signal. With these guys bridging the gap to identify what "Stay" means will require smooth hand cues and careful observation to beat the dog's 'movement' toward the treat.

The hand command, a one/two beat, and a reward before the dog moves, starts the learning process. We then repeat these steps, adding extra seconds before rewarding. Next we take a step or two away from the dog, returning with quick smooth actions to make full payments, before the dog breaks his stillness. As distance increases, expect the dog to fail the first time you turn your back, or go around a corner out of sight. To solve the problem, return the dog to its position and turn around sooner, and reward from a closer distance. Use a similar tack for going round the corner, go out of sight, then pop back into view with the hand signal present, extending the duration and distance as you go.

Wolters suggested a fun game for this stage of training. It involved getting the dog to 'stay' near one side of the house. Then, have him guess which side we're going to reappear from.

"Lying down" and "Staying" is work. Clients, with dogs that have high drives and short attention spans, are often advised to work on their dog's Long Down-Stays. They're encouraged to practice in their homes, starting with short durations and progressing to two hours.

"That's easy!" a lot of clients say. But, once they hear the rules they change their minds. The rules of a two hour down-stay are; they lay the dog down at the start of a movie, and two hours later, tell the dog he's finished work. If during the two hours, the dog gets up, we have to reset the timer. Sometimes, doing *Nothing* is harder than doing *Something*.

Heel - is one of the most challenging behaviours to teach. It's the act of linking a fixed location, their head beside our leg, in a moving environment. The round room is again the best place to begin.

Most dogs are taught to heel on the owner's left side, a left-over from days of old when hunting was more common. It was safest to keep the dog on the off side, of where the right handed shooter carried his gun. While walking along a road facing traffic, it puts the dog away from the vehicle lane, with our body as a buffer.

Food leading, by this time should be old hat.

Exaggerating the 'heel' position we want the dog to take is important, at the start. Watch an obedience trial and notice how unnatural the dogs look trotting along on a heel, their necks craned to look up at the handler. This exaggerated position asks the dog to watch only the trainer's face.

This position may not be too practical for a walk in forested areas, but by the time we get them out and about, we'll be able to relax the exaggerated position so they can watch where they're going. Starting with exaggerated posture, allows for the loosening of the reins, after the behaviour is conditioned, with the option of tightening them back up again at any time.

On busy city streets, it's more comfortable for passersby who may be afraid of dogs, if our animals are only making eye contact with us. Someone who is afraid of dogs has that fear multiplied, when eye contact is made with a <u>creature</u> that scares them. If our dog is anxious or fearful, seeing a passing stranger that's about ready to scream and run away isn't going to do much to calm them down either.

Start by putting the dog in position with food leading techniques, circling him around to whichever side you want him to be on. We'll set the dog's eyes and nose on the hand nearest them, which just happens to be holding a wonderful little hunk 'o byproducts in a tube. We'll bring our hand from their nose to a midway point between their eyes and ours, helping to create the 'eye-line' we want them to maintain. Giving the dog a visual clue for them to guess what we'll do next, we can lean our upper bodies forward a fraction of a second before we take a step. As the dog moves forward in position, start the hand moving back toward its mouth, as you say, "Good" to complete the full payment. Take one step, pay - three steps, pay - five steps, pay - ten steps, pay - and on and on. Keep in mind, that we want to 'pay' the dog for moving in a specific position, and for holding a particular posture. It takes practise to get the full payment into the dog's mouth while we're moving, walk slowly. It's okay to stop walking after a full payment. After each stop, use the same cue to resume walking.

Progress, to walking in circles away from the dog, then circles toward the dog. They're a predator, so walking slowly in the early stages, helps them avoid trying to initiate a game of "Catch the wiener". Ultimately, our cue for "Heel" can be minimized to tapping the side of our leg by using that motion as the first part of the food leading cue. Remember, the more the spoons clicked, the more eager we were. Frequent rewards, during the early stages of teaching "Heel," will save time and frustration down the road.

Obedience training provides valuable skills to the dog, and relieves many stressors, by developing the confidence and control that comes with repetition and positive training practices. The most valuable, often subliminal, benefit that arises from training any behaviour with our dogs, is the rapport that builds while doing the training. Rapport consists of trust, understanding, and acceptance of each other, which, after time, manifests as seamless control, whatever the situation. If we have a good rapport with our dogs, we'll be able to effortlessly predict what, how, when, and why they'll do things. This is precious in avoiding loss of control, as well as, in ensuring continued, positive, life, and training experiences for our maturity challenged charges.

Training with our dogs should never come to an end. We'll run out of ideas for new behaviours, before they'll be ready to stop learning.

Directional Commands

How to teach directional commands, is fun if we liken it to teaching our dogs a simplified version of baseball. By using a simple progression that starts by teaching the dog to go to a "mark." (This isn't the same as a bird dog's mark.) This kind of "mark" is like an actor's mark. Where the mark denotes a specific spot on the stage. Teaching this kind of "mark," should be a part of every progression plan we create and should be taught early on in their schooling.

The steps of the plan include:
- "Mark"
- "go to" mark
- "stop" on mark
- Multiple marks
- follow hand signals to indicated mark
- follow known cues while on mark

To start with we'll use a pedestal-type structure, big enough so that the dog can get up on it and lay down. It should be an easy step up, to begin with. At least four of five inches off the ground with good traction for the dog to stand on. As the dog progresses, the pedestal height can be adjusted in size. Eventually, the "mark" can be exchanged to a piece of wood or rock, just large enough for their front feet. Once they know the cue means to "Stand on

THIS spot," a dog with a good "mark" command can be moved about from one object to another, changing to "marks" of different sizes and shapes flawlessly.

With the dog free or tethered (whichever way makes it easiest for the dog to stay focussed), we'll food lead it around so that it stands opposite us with the pedestal in the middle. Entice the dog up onto the "mark" with food-leading techniques, timing the full payment with a big "Good" the moment that all four of the dog's feet land on the surface of the mark. The first few times, we can make the mark a doubly good thing by food-leading the dog off of it, making a full payment for following your cue to "get off."

Sometimes we'll need to do a lot of persuading to get the dog to step up off the ground. Ensuring the mark is firmly planted and doesn't wobble under weight helps minimize some dog's aversion to leaving the ground. Many will try to step around it, to get closer to us by any means possible - except stepping on the mark. Other dogs will just stand there and freeze up. Stimulating them to "Chase" the food we're leading with often helps get them "Un-stuck." If we reach over the mark and hold the food a little closer to their noses, we can then tease them to move a little one way and then the other, then back toward stepping up.

A rule I like to promote surrounding "marks" is that nothing physical should ever be done to them when they are on it, or to get them up on it. They should never be pulled up with a leash or have a foot pulled up into place.

We know we've done well teaching "mark" when we turn the dog out into the backyard for a pee and look out later to find that the dog is standing on it - his newest most favourite place in the world.

Once the dog is consistently getting up and down from the mark we can start sending them to it from our side. The dog should hop up and turn around to look back at us. From there we can bait the dog to the far side of the mark by tossing a treat a short way. When they are finished and head back to us for more goodies, we can cue them to mark and have them "stop" on it before getting all the way to us. This can be a tricky step if the dog is moving fast. In these cases we need to cue the "mark" first and then time the "stay" command after the dog has committed to going to the "mark." Being able to stop them on a mark from a run is a small triumph.

From this stage we can introduce another pedestal to act as 'second base.' After acclimating the dog to the new mark, it should be an easy step, to have the dog go between either of the two. Start this step with the marks a few feet apart. Once they've gone between the two pedestals a few times, we can increase the distance between them rapidly,from four or five feet to twenty or more.

The addition of a third "mark" completes our 'ball diamond' and readies the dog for the final steps in our directional command progression plan.

Moving into "directional commands" from one layer

"go to" or "stopping" on a mark is achieved by placing the dog where 'home plate' would be, make it stay and walk out onto the imaginary pitcher's mound. Using "big pointing" hand cues we can direct them to either First or Third base without too much confusion. If there is a hesitation from the dog at this stage, we can help by taking a step toward the base we're sending them to, as an add-on to the hand signal. From this set up the dog is blocked from Second base by our body, so we'll save that one for after they've done a few runs to First and Third.

Standing beside the dog on home plate and sending it out to one of the three marks or bases is the next natural step in their progression, followed by starting the dog on the pitcher's mound and directing them from home plate to either of the marks. From there on out, it's just a matter of adding distance to create that, "Remote controlled dog" most of us only see on t.v. or at retrieval trials. The more successful 'sends' we have, the quicker and more eager the dog will be to add distance to this set of commands.

Once we've got the non-verbal cues out of the way and understood by the dog we can start adding either spoken or whistle commands to our visual cues. Whistles travel farther and don't carry emotion, They are best to use for dogs that will work at great distances.

Using Routines:

As mentioned earlier, consistency is essential in some forms, but can have its drawbacks in others by creating unwanted routines.

Routines are essential to use when we come up with jobs for our dogs that require multiple small steps. Routines provide the vehicle for some of the most intricate and amazing feats we can develop with our dogs.

Benny was a master of routines. He was happy to form them, or discard them, in turn for another. He was a Lab/Rottweiler cross whose most popular trick was getting a pop from the fridge.

When my Son, was a toddler and learned he could open the fridge door, he became the inspiration for Benny to learn this trick. Benny knew what "close the door" meant, so when Connor decided he would stand at the fridge and open and close it, I thought, "Hmmm this might be a cool parenting innovation".

I had Benny come around and stand where he could close it.

When Connor pulled the door open, I'd cue Benny to "close it". Benny looked from me to Connor, and then to the door. He picked up his foot, half-heartedly, and pushed it closed.

Little Connor wasn't too firm on his feet yet, and the novelty of reaching up and grabbing the handle to open the fridge was a consuming task. It took a couple rounds before he realized Benny was closing the door, and not some mysterious door function he hadn't figured out yet.

Benny was familiar with and liked, pushing doors of all kinds closed. He'd usually perk up his flop ears and bounce a little, showing his anticipation to "do it again!" But, this scenario made him a little nervous. Connor was little, but he was a human nonetheless. Connor's full attention was focused on the fridge door and handle, and to Benny's perception, I was asking him to take, or push, the door away from Connor. Benny wasn't sure that was a very <u>Proper</u> thing to do to someone who wasn't asking for, nor wanting, to play with him.

After five or six rounds of toddler vs dog, Benny assumed he mustn't be doing the right thing. The next time I told him to "close it" he tried something different. He took hold of the handle and pulled the door wide open. Connor and Benny both thought that HAD to be the perfect move!

I was foiled! But it did give me a good idea for what to do next.

I tied a dishcloth to the fridge's door handle and taught Benny to "open' the door! After he was consistently opening the fridge door by pulling on the towel, we switched to something else.

I pulled a can from the fridge and had Benny do a few 'careful' retrieves, with the can first placed on the floor, then on the seat of a chair, then beside the left-over chicken in the fridge.

After that, it was just a matter of joining the two things together: "open the door" and "bring me a pop." After he'd brought the pop, he was asked to go back and "close the door".

The whole lesson took no more than fifteen or twenty minutes. Benny already had a solid foundation of basic commands, as well as forced and blind retrieves. So it was just a matter of tweaking what he already knew, putting it into a new routine that was eventually called "Get me a Pepsi".

Training 'new' routines can be fun and useful. But routine and consistency can mutate, if improperly used.

A dog with an anxious disposition can be susceptible to elevated stress, when long-held routines are not maintained. The number of dogs being medicated for separation anxiety, should be our first a clue. The way to avoid such doldrums is to be fluid in our routines, always changing, adding, or removing things, places, and times of doing things.

Discipline:

Most people notice that Discipline is a somewhat marginalized topic, throughout our sessions. The reason for that is based on another Therrien-ism "*If you have to make a correction to an animal for its behaviour, it's because we are screwing up, not the animal*".

In terms of what we've discussed in developing an honest and true perspective of being the dog's Mother, discipline is simply the varied tones of "No", which indicates to the dog when its actions or behaviours are inappropriate.

The use of physical corrections such as with a jerk on a leash to make a dog "heel," make no sense to our dog's and exacerbate resistance and confusion. There are times when our young dogs may get a "out of control" during play or in exciting new environments, but turning their behaviour into a negative with a correction, only stands to create a negative association with the game or environment. There are times when for safety sake we might have to restrain our dogs actions, but doing so from a place of positive intent and with open eyes is the best course.

"Never pick a fight you can't win." is a good adage in this regard. Many times people will perceive a 'problem' when from the dog's perspective things are just exciting or interesting. The 'fight' in this old saying shouldn't be taken as a literal - brawl - but as a difference in perspective that we've failed to clarify.

Our own emotions must remain in check, when we feel the need to *discipline* our dogs. Rage-filled corrections destroy relationships, whereas corrections made with proper tone and timing can solidify trust and guide the animal to clearer perspectives. If our dogs misbehave, we should first ask ourselves what we have done wrong.

With all these conglomerated truths bouncing around in our heads, it's time to let it soak in and start experimenting with how all this sits in our brain, and how our dogs will soak it up into theirs.

CHAPTER SIX

Final Truths

Diet

From their humble roots, canines evolved as omnivores, suited to a varied diet of carrion, fresh meat, fruits, grasses and vegetables.

Today, store-bought pet foods range the full spectrum, from human grade organic ingredients, to cute little squares baked from a battered gruel of corn and ground chicken feathers flavoured with savoury... *stuff*. The pet food aisle in grocery stores are mini versions of the human wares up for sale. With corn, fat, sugar, and salt making up the majority of tonnage hauled in by trucks and out in baskets.

Stores specializing in pet foods offer meat selections that rival butcher shops: beef, chicken, fish, and lamb, with some high-end stores offering: buffalo, duck, and venison to their menus. If the Dogs of old could see them now!

* * *

Far from being a canine nutritionalist, I encourage diligent pet owners to research for themselves to find a diet and appropriate feeding regime that suits their lives and their dog's needs. There are many resources out there to help the novice pet owner decide. A veterinarian who advocates a raw-food diet can be a huge help.

The diet we feed our pets can play a significant role in their behaviour. Some dog's are sensitive to different foods, much the same as people are. One of the more common effects of diet are seen when a dog is fed an excess of red meat such as Beef, buffalo or venison. The high protein levels in red meat tend to "rev-up" a dog's activity levels. In much the same way as feeding grain to a horse, or chocolate to a child. In short: too much red meat can be like trying to control a kid who has been fed sugar and chocolate bars for breakfast. With unruly dogs, sometimes it's just a matter of reducing the amount of red meat they eat by switching to chicken, fish or pork based foods.

Tessa the little cocker from past stories, is one who shows an immediate response to too much red meat. Her owner noticed marked difference in her behaviour when we discussed the effects of red meat and he cut her back as a result. To this day he gauges her red meat intake by how "bitchy" she is toward people and other dogs. Cutting her back when she starts showing her nasty-side too much.

There has been very little published research on the effects of diet and behaviour but like many bits of common sense and logic the proof is in the pudding - or the meat pie - as the case may be.

Stress

It's not uncommon for canine behaviour issues to originate from biological processes gone awry. Thyroid disease, tumours, hormonal imbalances and gastric irregularities to name a few. There have been many puzzling behaviours that were linked to pathological issues that once treated resolved the behavioural issue.

Other behaviours can be seen to accompany or fore-shadow disease. A common vein in health concerns with diseases such as demodetic mange, many skin sensitivities and irritable bowel problems can be related directly back to stress from the animal's perception of the world or rather, their unclear perspectives.

Stress is now globally acknowledged as having many detrimental effects on the human body. This acknowledgement comes after a multitude of clinical studies on animals and humans that, 'revealed' what sage health practitioners had intuited millennia ago. Stress is bad for us. One of the global acknowledgements on the effects of stress is that anxiety can suppress the immune system, leaving it open to attack from all kinds of nasty things.

Demodetic mange can be a horrific plight for dogs and their owners. The disease is caused by a naturally occurring mite. In some cases these mites are able to over come the body's natural defence mechanisms and an outbreak occurs. The mites can cause hair loss, secondary bacterial skin infections, and at the generalized stage, pustules, edema and swelling. The cure is often a barrage of insecticides administered orally, often requiring long rounds of treatment, with guarded prognosis for some.

One year seemed to send this connection my way to drive home the point. It started with a long time client and acquaintance bringing her new dog by for an assessment. The dog didn't take to me at all when she introduced us, which surprised both of us. After watching the dog move around and respond to the different stimuli on the farm, I asked her to tie him on a long line to a tree, then we both moved away from him.

After a short time I approached him again, without his human being in the mix. My luck was no better convincing him of my benign intent than it had been before he was tied. Yet, his body language depicted a mix of contrasting emotions. In his own way he was saying that he didn't want to be stranded by the tree all alone and that he was interested in me as a potential ally - but he didn't want me too close to him. His mixed signals seemed to be a step up from when he'd first arrived so I backed off and gave him room again. Standing back beside his owner I watched the dog a little longer and was struck with a thought.

I asked her "Has he ever had any skin problems? Hair loss?"

* * *

She gave me a questioning look and answered "No." She then quickly followed up with "But he does have a small patch under his eye."

After a time the dog settled enough for her to hold him while I got in to take a closer look at the 'patch' she'd noticed. Contrary to normal presentation with mange the dog had a small circular patch of thinning hair under his right eye, hardly noticeable. Mange will typically start on the upper eyelid/eyebrow region and spread from there.

"Why?" she asked next.

I answered that her dog wasn't acting normally, even for one that didn't like me. I told her that for whatever reason he was giving me the same signals that I'd noticed with other dogs who had suffered from generalized demodetic mange. He wanted attention but didn't trust me to touch him, in order to get it. We decided that he should come and hang out for a few days or a week to give me time to get to know him better and give her a better read on her dog. At the time, Benny, my old Lab/Rottie cross was getting very old. I asked her if she'd mind taking the dog in for a skin scraping at the vets to make sure it was mange and not ring-worm (which given the patch's location and shape - seemed more likely than mange). I didn't want to subject old Ben to ring-worm at his age, but didn't think he'd be affected by contact with a dog who was having an outbreak of mange, given that it is not considered 'catchy' except from mothers to pups.

She agreed, but said "Chris, my vet, is going to think

we're nuts - I just had him in to see her a few days ago."

I told her why I was worried and what to tell the vet when she asked.

When she'd seen the vet, she returned with the dog and a question from the vet that we both knew very well. She told how Chris the vet had scoffed at first, but once she'd been told why I didn't want to bring the dog into my house with ring-worm, and that I'd guessed that it might be mange her curiosity took over and she agreed to the test. She said Chris took the scraping and left the exam room to have a look under the microscope. When she returned to the room with the results she'd asked her "How did he know?"

Two more dog's came along that summer with the same kind of issues, caused by the same undiagnosed over abundance of mange mites. None of the dogs presented with visible hair-loss which is the typical, first sign of infection. All of the dogs presented with varying degrees of aggression and atypical levels of anxiety in their countenance.

They all came from good homes that provided good food and veterinary care. All three recovered without treatment for mites, by changing them and their owner's perspectives about The Dog's Honest Truth.

May you enjoy good timing, understanding, and *The Dog's Honest Truth*.

* * *

The End

www.ingramcontent.com/pod-product-compliance
Lightning Source LLC
Chambersburg PA
CBHW031829090426
42741CB00005B/185